Leadership

The Art of Inspiring People to Be Their Best

Kellan,

I hope you find
something in here of value
as you climb your own mountain!

Craig Wheldan

Leadership

The Art of Inspiring People to Be Their Best

MAJOR GENERAL CRAIG B. WHELDEN

U.S. ARMY (RETIRED)

New Insights Press

Published by New Insights Press, Los Angeles, CA

Editorial Direction: Rick Benzel
Editing: Rick Benzel
Cover Design: Josep Book Designs
Book Design: Josep Book Designs

Printed in the United States of America
ISBN: 978-1-7338411-3-9 (print)
ISBN: 978-0-9984850-5-8 (ebook)

Library of Congress Control Number: 2019936526

Dedicated to my dad...

...who inspired me at an early age to climb my own mountain and to be my best.

1st Lieutenant George T. Whelden Jr. – 1944

Testimonials

"Before reading a book on leadership, examine the life, character and career of the author. Then ask yourself, 'Did he walk the walk? Does he have the character to deserve your trust? Did he have a career worthy of such a substantial investment of your time?' For Craig Whelden, the answer is yes, yes, and yes."

Pete Geren, former Secretary of the Army

★ ★ ★

"This is a classic piece of work. Craig Whelden has crafted, in a profound and masterful way, a set of real-world leadership thoughts from his own experiences that go well beyond a description of the past. You'll find that these lessons have universal application in the private sector as well."

GENERAL Gordon Sullivan, U.S. Army (Retired),
32nd Army Chief of Staff

★ ★ ★

"Craig Whelden is in a select group of the most brilliant general officers ever produced by the Army. He is a master leader and his book lays it all out. It's classic Whelden and will be a bedrock leadership staple for decades."

GENERAL B. B. Bell, U.S. Army (Retired);
former Commander, U.S. Army, Europe;
NATO's Land Component; U.S./Allied Forces, Korea

★ ★ ★

"Craig Whelden is a leader soldiers have wanted to follow his entire career. Anyone wanting to develop their leadership potential or who seek to build a high performing team should listen to his sage advice and learn from his experiences."

GENERAL David McKiernan, U.S. Army (Retired)

"I've known Craig Whelden for more than 30 years and have found him to be one of the most inspirational leaders with whom I have served within my 39-year career in the U.S. Army. Trust is one of the most important traits a leader must possess, and Craig personifies trust."

GENERAL James D. (JD) Thurman, U.S. Army (Retired),
former Commander, U.S./Allied Forces, Korea

★ ★ ★

"If you believe good leaders never stop learning, you will love this book. Craig has artfully captured lifelong lessons that contributed to his success as a leader, professional, and wonderful human being."

GENERAL Ann Dunwoody, U.S. Army (Retired),
America's first female four-star general

★ ★ ★

"If you want to get a huge head start on your leadership journey read this book at an early point in your career, whether in the public or private sector. It will impact greatly how you approach each challenge at every level of responsibility."

ADMIRAL Tom Fargo, U.S. Navy (Retired) –
former Commander, U.S. Pacific Command

★ ★ ★

"I am privileged to have witnessed first-hand the 'Whelden Leadership Model' in several different, challenging assignments I shared with Craig. He is singularly qualified to provide his thoughts on leadership. Spanning over four decades of brilliant service to our Nation, Craig has been at the forefront of innovative thinking, inspirational counsel, and abiding concern for the health and welfare of those in his charge."

ADMIRAL Timothy J. Keating, U.S. Navy (Retired) –
former Commander, U.S. Pacific Command and former Commander,
U.S. Northern Command

"Major General Craig Whelden has written a must-read primer on leadership. Read this book and learn from one of the best."

Sergeant Major of the Army Jack L. Tilley, U.S. Army (Retired)

★ ★ ★

"Craig Whelden is an inspirational leader who truly cares about people. I always admired his leadership and tried to be like him. Craig has done a magnificent job in this book capturing the essence of engaged leadership and highlighting specific examples of its application through the use of personal stories and vignettes. Highly recommended for anyone who aspires to be a better leader... and that should be all of us."

Lieutenant General Rick Lynch, US Army (Retired).
Author of *Adapt or Die: Battle Tested Principles for Leaders* and *Work Hard, Pray Hard: The Power of Faith in Action.*

★ ★ ★

"General Whelden has spent his entire adult life successfully leading, inspiring, and motivating people and organizations to change, become better and accomplish things they never thought possible. Learn from someone who really understands and has practiced the principles of leadership for 40+ years! Read this book!"

Lieutenant General Henry T. Glisson, U.S. Army (Retired)

★ ★ ★

"General Whelden's wisdom and experience as a leader—dedicated to inspiring the best efforts from those in his charge—provides a needed corrective to the toxic leadership all too common in our national life. This is a valuable guide to thriving in tough times."

Lieutenant General Wallace "Chip" Gregson, USMC (Retired),
Former Commander, U.S. Marine Corps Forces Pacific

"In the more than 15 years I have worked with Army and Marine Corps leader Craig Whelden, it's his ability to clearly communicate complex, multi-faceted issues to a variety of audiences that has been most impressive."

Jennifer Sabas, Chief of Staff for Daniel K. Inouye, former U.S. Senator and Medal of Honor recipient

★　★　★

"In the years following 9/11, I was honored to have Craig organize and chair multiple conferences that our company produced on Information Sharing and Homeland Security. All were huge successes. Craig inspired thousands of leaders from the Intelligence Community, the Department of Defense, law enforcement, the private sector, academia, and industry to gather face-to-face to find better ways to win the war on terrorism!"

John Skipper, President, National Conference Services, Inc.

*"What the Marine Corps taught me can
be seen every day in FedEx"*

Frederick W. Smith

Chairman and CEO, FedEx Corporation

Table of Contents

Foreword

What Now, Lieutenant?

More than 50 years ago while studying to be an Army officer, our class had a series of films to watch, titled, "What Now, Lieutenant?" Each short film would present a scenario during which the young and inexperienced lieutenant would face a challenge—a crisis of command—in which his soldiers would literally look to him for resolution. The instructor would stop the projector (remember, this was 50 years ago) and then ask for the answer.

We would occasionally get it right, but we always got the lesson: that good leaders must make good decisions for good reasons. I can still recall the exact details of the particular episode that stuck with me throughout my career. I think it was my first brush with learning about leadership.

I have known Craig Whelden for more than 20 years and have watched him in action as an Army General Officer and as a Senior Executive for the Marine Corps. As I read his book, I was reminded again of how much one can learn about leadership through watching others grapple with the demands of leadership and how each of them acts, makes decisions, and does not shy from accountability. We learn most from successful leaders, because we see what works and why. Craig is one such leader, and his ability to share his experiences—some of which are intensely personal—and articulate what he has learned enriches the reader.

The chapters are short, with intriguing titles. They contain several vignettes from his life with pertinent leadership examples and lessons. He is very clear in explaining each challenge, and he is equally straight-forward in explaining his solution. You'll gain a valuable perspective on style and substance through his experiences. He is not pedantic... he is conversational. You will come away with guidelines and principles that mark a leader who others want to follow.

Craig provides compelling examples of leading units through change and turbulence. In fact, his leadership journey is also a biography of the American Army in one of its most transformative periods, 1973-2003, the exact 30 years Craig went from 2nd lieutenant to major general. He saw the agonizing recovery from the Vietnam War, the elimination of the draft, the training revolution, the success of the volunteer force, the rise of the joint force, and the nation again at war. Those who served during that period will find themselves remembering the many challenges that surfaced as the Army and the nation regained its footing after Vietnam. We owe Craig and his generation of officers our profound gratitude for what they accomplished in leading the Army from turbulence to triumph.

Yes, this is a book about successful leadership in a military environment. But, in virtually every vignette, one can extrapolate the essence and apply lessons to the corporate world, the not-for-profit world, or even the arena of leading volunteers. There is a lot here for every leader, neophyte or experienced. I suggest those serving or who have served will find themselves very easily in the book, and each may be able to compare their leadership experience to how Craig approached the challenge.

For me, the chapters on character, loyalty, virtual mentorship, ethics (*Memento Mori*) and hope (*The Light at the End of the Tunnel*) especially resonated. No surprise, Chapter 1 is about character; we know it's the prerequisite for all effective leaders. Craig points out that loyalty is both a process and an investment. You'll be surprised when you read the key to his getting the Senior Executive Service (SES) position with the Marine Corps, despite the odds. I have often argued for the under-appreciated value of the role model in leader development, but Craig elevates it properly in his unique take on *virtual* mentorship, with his four categories of mentors. I would have every senior executive, military and civilian, read *Memento Mori*, both for the examples and the lessons.

As I mentioned, Craig does not blanch when addressing the challenge of leading in the midst of personal setback and profound tragedy. He inspires here by baring his life and showing how a leader retains equilibrium while leading others, realizing there is a light—elusive in the moment—but still there at the end of the tunnel. Craig brings the cliché to life.

Every reader will find their own special chapters, as I did. If you want an executive summary, read Appendix A, *Whelden Philosophy of Command*. He was and is as good as his words. I know as I've watched and admired him as a leader, husband, and father.

Now, here's a leadership vignette Craig did not provide: This past November my wife and I attended the annual Marine Corps Birthday Ball. Also in attendance were Marine Corps senior leaders, including Craig. After dinner, when the informal comradery took hold, groups of Marines gathered for photos. One large group of Marines of all ranks gathered in front of the large American flag, and they called for one man to join them. They had a choice of many senior Marines, but they chose Craig. There he stood with the Marines, unique in his civilian clothes, and the one they chose. Here was a leader who had gained their respect, admiration, and affection.

For 39 years, Craig has been the leader others want to follow. This book will surely add to the legacy of leadership he has left through his impact on others by inspiring them, and those who follow, to be their best.

David A. Bramlett
GENERAL, US Army (Retired)
Former Commander, US Army Forces Command

Prologue

Webster defines leadership as *"the act or an instance of leading."* If there's one profession where strong and effective leadership is absolutely required, it is the military.

Exceptional corporate leadership is, of course, also a necessity, focused on maximizing profits, producing high quality products, and keeping a company sustainable. Leadership in government, too, is critical, moving society forward and guiding the ongoing process of democracy.

But military leadership is different. It is about ensuring a nation's survival, preventing its decline, or, worst case, its demise. It is about life and death.

I've spent most of my life in or around the military. I was an Air Force family member growing up, then had a 30-year career as an Army officer and another nine years as a member of the federal government's Senior Executive Service (SES) with the Marine Corps.

Combined, I spent 16 years as either an Army General Officer or a Marine Corps Senior Executive, providing ample opportunity to develop my own leadership skills. Over the course of the past many decades, I worked for some brilliant and highly effective leaders and learned a great deal about what made them tick. I saw how they inspired people to be their best and I hope to have picked up some of their habits.

I've also worked for some not-so-great leaders and have learned from them, as well: what not to do.

My purpose in writing this book is to "pay forward" those lessons: both good and bad. I entitled the book *Leadership: The Art of Inspiring People to Be Their Best* because I believe this is precisely the key to great leadership—helping people perform at their best.

My five decades of experience should be relevant and helpful to leaders and aspiring leaders in *any* profession—as well as in their personal lives. You will also find this book an interesting and fun read because I move beyond the dryness and banality of academic theory, citing personal examples about what has worked for me... and what has not. As they say in Hawaii, we are going to *"talk story."*

Before delving into the main part of the book, let me state the obvious. Leading is complicated. Many tangible and intangible qualities are found in both leaders and those being led that—when combined—contribute to the overall effectiveness of a good leader. Getting people to follow you is a function of inspiring the loyalty of those being led, and understanding what expectations THEY have of the type of leader they are willing to follow.

In effect, there is a mutual dependence in the relationship, forged through trust, shared values, and mutually desired goals. It is as much art as science. Hence, the subtitle of this book: *"The **Art** of Inspiring People to Be Their Best."*

Many may think that the military relies on a disciplined set of rules to have effective leaders, but make that the first lesson of this book. While the military does instill strict rules and regulations on its uniformed members, the tenets of strong leadership are not built on that foundation alone. Members of the military are neither robots nor automatons. They are living, feeling human beings, just like corporate employees or members of any organization. They pay taxes, raise families, and live in our communities. They have both personal and professional issues that need attending to. Paying attention to their emotional, psychological, and spiritual needs, along with their professional development, is critical if you want them to willingly and unfailingly follow you.

In the course of this book, you will learn much about my approach to leadership, and about me. I hope the lessons I have carved out from the past 50 years will help you improve your leadership skills and inspire you to be the best you can be in whatever you do.

Not every chapter includes a leadership lesson... though most do. Some chapters have very clear lessons, others are subtle, and some are just a fun ride. Agree or disagree, keep what you want, and disregard what you've already mastered or what isn't a good personal fit for you.

It's all free – after you purchase the book!

Finally, I hope that you too will "pay forward" to others whatever you think is worthy.

1

Character: Leadership's Basic Building Block

"Talent is God given. Be humble. Fame is man-given.
Be grateful. Conceit is self-given. Be careful."

John Wooden

There has been a long-running debate about whether great leaders are born that way or are developed through experience, education and training. I suggest that both are required. No one doubts that the very best leaders have both innate and developed skills, built upon through education and experience. But the greatest talents and experts do not always make great leaders.

A critical and foundational element of the very best leaders is *character*, with qualities like ambition, perseverance, self-awareness, empathy, humility, integrity, and always taking seriously the responsibility of being a leader… often while sacrificing their own personal welfare or gain.

Character is part nature, part nurture. It obviously helps to be born with the right genetic makeup that predisposes you to be a great leader. However, I've seen too many people who thought they were "born leaders," while nature didn't agree. They didn't nurture what little they had to fill the gaps. They lacked the qualities cited above and seemed to operate solely on raw instinct. Some led by commanding others loudly, harshly, and aggressively. They may have believed the only way to get results was with an iron fist.

Others I've known have taken advantage of their position of power, imposing their will through brute techniques and hardly inspiring others. The *MeToo* movement has brought that approach into the national consciousness in spades.

> *Combining innate skills with world-class training quite often produces great results. The U.S. military seeks the former and provides the latter.*

I've also seen people who were born into tremendous adversity and had little leadership training, yet they nurtured their best qualities and became leaders who can attract followers as few others can. Combining innate skills with world-class training quite often produces great results. The U.S. military seeks the former and provides the latter. The result has been tested in some of the most difficult circumstances throughout our nation's history and has produced a stable of exceptional leaders when our nation needed them most.

Let me delve more into the qualities of character I think leaders need to have and how nature can be nurtured to produce the best of breed. Even if you don't consider yourself a "born leader," effective training and experience can produce great results. Leadership can be taught, as long as there are basic building blocks already there.

Ambition & Perseverance

Behind every great leader are these two strong character traits. Ambition is what drives them to excel, to have a vision of better results, and to strive for personal excellence in everything they do. Perseverance is what keeps them going any time they encounter an obstacle or challenge that seems like it will block forward progress. Some call this "grit."

These qualities were first instilled in me by my dad. He too was in the military, and his story is worth sharing.

George Whelden was a sophomore at Purdue University in 1941. On December 7th of that year—a lazy Sunday afternoon—he was walking up the stairs of his fraternity trying to decide whether to study or go see a movie when he overheard from a nearby room a radio report of the attack on Pearl Harbor. The very next day, he and most of his fraternity brothers went to the recruiting office to "sign up," but—overwhelmed by the sheer volume of volunteers—the recruiters told them to go back to school and wait until called, as there wasn't enough capacity to train the millions who wanted to enlist. When he was finally called several months later, he ended up in flight school in Texas, followed by a posting to India where he flew C47s into Kunming, China in support of Chenault's Flying Tigers.

After the war, my dad returned to the U.S. to resume his education at Indiana University's law school. In 1948, he married my mother, Mary "Joan" Beckett. A year later my brother was born, and in 1951, I followed. Just months before my father was to take the bar exam, the Korean War broke out. He was recalled to active duty and sent to Fort Benning to support the Army's Airborne School (a school I attended 20 years later).

From that initial assignment, and now with a wife and two kids in tow, he decided to stay in the Air Force after the Korean War and, for the next 20 years, my family traveled all over the world: Georgia, Oklahoma, Colorado, England, New Mexico, Alabama, Louisiana, Paris, France; and finally, Casteau, Belgium.

At Bossier Air Force Base, near Shreveport, Louisiana, he worked for a man who was incorrigible. Not only did he have him as his boss for the entire three years we were there, but this man was also our next door neighbor. Their personalities were like oil and water, and it was a low point for my dad because there was no escape. Through it all, he persevered.

He had "grit."

Fortunately, a former mentor from our time in England reached out to help facilitate his next assignment to Paris, France, where my dad joined the Supreme Headquarters for Allied Powers Europe (SHAPE), the military arm of the North Atlantic Treaty Organization (NATO). A year later, President Charles de Gaulle pulled France out of NATO and we left Paris on short notice. Southern Belgium became our new home and it was where I spent my last two years of high school.

My dad retired from the Air Force just as I was starting college in the early '70s. He returned to law school, but it had been such a long time since he was a law student that he had to start over. He was given credit for only one course: *Introduction to Law*. With classes at night and a day job as a county clerk, he still managed to graduate cum laude in just a few years, and he eventually became a judge for the state of Indiana.

Becoming a lawyer was something my dad wanted as long as I can remember. Watching him persevere through those hard times in Louisiana, and watching his laser focus on this ultimate goal, I was inspired at an early age to "climb my own mountain…"

…to be the "best I can be."

Self-Awareness

I suggest that great leaders also possess a subtle quality called self-awareness. In today's parlance, they have a high degree of mindfulness. They can examine their thoughts and actions and almost intuitively recognize when they are on the right path… or the wrong one. They know themselves well, and are sensitive and cognizant of how others view them.

My own self-awareness started to take shape when I attended the Army's Ranger School in 1973. This superb training and leadership school used peer reviews to help weed out candidates who are not good team players. We were required to rate each other on many qualities, which is a sure-fire way to become self-aware. I next encountered a similar peer review technique only when I became a General Officer 23 years later. It was incorporated into an annual questionnaire that asked three questions about every officer of the same rank:

- *Do you know this officer?*
- *If yes, do you recommend this officer for promotion?*
- *If yes, do you recommend this officer for command?*

I dutifully filled out the questionnaire every year and forwarded it back to the source, where it presumably was folded into an algorithm and provided to the Chief of Staff of the Army, who used it to help him select his General Officers for assignments and command.

The only other instance of such an introspective review for me started in 2010 when I became a member of the federal government's Senior Executive Service, a position I held for more than nine years. Every three years, we were required to take a 360-degree evaluation which solicits input from our boss, our contemporaries, and our subordinates ... all (except the boss) done anonymously. The evaluation was extensive, asking many questions and leaving room for comments. It also asked that we rate ourselves, so we could see how our view compared to how others see us.

It is important for leaders to be self-aware, while equally appreciating how they are viewed by others based on job knowledge, dedication to the team, empathy, optimism, character, humility, trust, approachability, and confidence. When combined, and if all these traits are positive, they inspire others. Exceptional leaders have the ability to motivate in a way that many others cannot. It's an intangible quality that raises the

> *Exceptional leaders have the ability to motivate in a way that many others cannot. It's an intangible quality that raises the probability of their success because people actually WANT to do well for them.*

probability of their success because people actually WANT to do well for them. An obvious byproduct is that it is also good for the organization as the organization becomes more productive.

I once worked for a 3-star general who was exceptionally smart, extremely competent, and the consummate gentleman. He never raised his voice in anger. One day, a colonel on our staff told me that the general was the *"toughest boss he had ever worked for."* Perplexed, I asked him why. He replied: *"Because I never wanted to disappoint him."*

I knew exactly what he meant.

A Positive Attitude

Having a positive attitude is a critical element of leadership. To some, this comes naturally. Others must constantly work on it. Since my earliest memory, I have had the sense that anything worth doing... worth pursuing... must be passionately pursued. A positive attitude naturally follows.

I found myself first assuming leadership responsibilities at age 14 when I became an Eagle Scout. Perhaps I was naïve, but the leadership aspect of this achievement was unexpected. For me, getting there was just a mountain to climb. It was the culmination of 21 merit badges and a large community project. It was the excitement of the journey, the arrival at a destination, and the achievement of the reward.

Eagle Scout - 1965

For me, at 14 years old, it was like reaching the top of Mount Everest but with no real thought (or plan) on how I was going to get back down… the part of the climb where most people die. Once there, I didn't quite know what to do with these newfound responsibilities when people started turning to me to lead. But it did help jump-start a lifelong journey to develop and sharpen my leadership skills—a journey that really never ends.

Great leaders constantly deal with the struggle between achieving personal goals, while doing so with humility. Ask yourself, "Do you want to achieve lofty goals in order to 'climb the mountain' or do you want to get on top of the mountain so that you can help others climb their own mountain?" How can you do both?

In high school, I held leadership roles in school government and on the sports field. In my senior year, I was voted *"Best All-Around"* and *"Most Dependable"*—the latter accolade drawing raised eyebrows from my parents! At Purdue University, I was President of the Freshman Council at the largest school dormitory, President of my Fraternity Pledge Class, and Vice President of Purdue's Interfraternity Council. (I ran for President, but was asked by the Council whether I would take the VP spot if not selected to be President. My agreement sealed my fate).

All these experiences helped shape my thinking about, and commitment to, leadership because people started to turn to me to lead. I had the right *attitude* throughout these early years. However, there came a period in college when I lost my way.

My attendance at Purdue was facilitated by an Army ROTC scholarship, at a time when the Vietnam War was stoking nationwide protests across nearly every college campus. Compared to other campuses, Purdue was a fairly conservative school, but we had a chapter of the Students for Democratic Society (SDS), and they regularly protested the war on the mall or at the Armory.

I had mixed feelings about the war when I arrived at Purdue in

1969, having spent most of my high school years in Europe—insulated from the anti-war movement. But since I had an ROTC scholarship and my dad was retiring from the Air Force and starting law school about the same time I entered college, I felt an obligation to stay in a program that was paying my way. I also worked 4 hours each evening (Monday - Friday) as a janitor, cleaning the second floor of the university library to help make ends meet.

Working as a Night Janitor at Purdue - 1970

Then an unfortunate event happened.

Because of my student government activities, my leadership role in the fraternity, and my work schedule (combined with ambivalence about the war), I didn't participate in any ROTC activities outside the classroom. Just walking across campus in uniform to attend military drills drew unwanted attention. So, when the annual Army ROTC awards ceremony occurred in the spring of my freshman year (1970), and knowing that I was not an award recipient, I decided to skip the ceremony and attend the SDS rally in the mall instead.

Not my brightest moment…

That day, after chanting *"1-2-3-4, we don't want your F*#king War!"*

over and over again, a growing crowd of about 1,000 decided to march on the Armory, where the ROTC awards ceremony had been moved to insulate it from the protests.

I followed the crowd.

Upon arriving at the armory, they broke open the large truck-sized doors and entered, chanting loud and strong. State troopers in riot gear soon arrived to keep the protesters away from the formation of cadets.

I was not an active protest participant, and naïvely thought of myself as being in some kind of "intellectual exercise," but one of my instructors saw me, that day. He called me in the following morning and told me that my scholarship was being put on probation.

This was a wakeup call for me, and it began the reshaping of my attitude. I had to decide which side to be on. I came to realize that I wanted to be a leader more than a protestor. Like some other Americans, I may have thought that the Vietnam War was ill-advised, but I also realized that there were alternative ways to make my mark on the world.

When ROTC summer camp training rolled around between my junior and senior year, I spent nine weeks at Fort Riley and did well enough to become the third ranking cadet at Purdue during my senior year. Upon graduation from Purdue in 1973, I was one of six cadets designated a *Distinguished Military Graduate*.

So, what should you take from this ROTC experience? In a nutshell: attitude counts.

A lot.

There's something to be said about the off-repeated mantra that *"you can be whatever you want to be."* That said, all aspects of character mentioned at the beginning of this chapter are required if you're to be the best you can be. You need building blocks to realize that dream. During those early years at Purdue—at least as it applied to an Army career—I lacked ambition, a good self-awareness, and perseverance.

I lacked "grit."

I simply knew that I owed four years to the Army after graduation because of my scholarship, but after that, I thought I could move on to something else. Once I finally decided to "get on board," my ambition, perseverance, and self-awareness kicked into high gear.

I then adjusted my attitude, and a 4-year commitment turned into a 30-year career.

2

Trusting Your People

"Few things help an individual more than
to place responsibility upon him, and to
let him know that you trust him."
Booker T. Washington

I n the first three years of my Army career, I was stationed at Fort
Hood, Texas. When my time there was to end, I was a first lieutenant, getting ready for my next assignment. I called my assignment officer in Washington DC to inquire about what was next.

Major Tom Montgomery answered the phone, and he seemed to be
in a bad mood. The first thing he said was how upset he was that Purdue
had just bested Indiana University in the *Old Oaken Bucket* football
game—the premier rivalry in the state of Indiana—the previous weekend. How did he know I was a graduate of Purdue, and why would
he be so concerned about a football game? As it turned out, he was a
graduate of Indiana and was just having some fun (at my expense)—the
beginning of banter between us that continues to this today.

After we got past this uncomfortable opening moment (for me,
at least), he confirmed that I was being assigned to Germany after I

attended the Armor Officers Advanced Course at Fort Knox. Then he casually suggested that, on my way to Germany, I should consider passing through Washington D.C. I asked if I could bring a friend, and he readily agreed.

My friend was Bob Westholm. He and I had been in the Armor Officer Basic Course together in 1973 and were placed on the same tank for training, since assignments were made alphabetically (Westholm, Whelden, Williams and Williams). Bob and I were then coincidentally sent to the same tank battalion at Fort Hood, Texas, and now, three years later, we would both be attending the Advanced Course at Fort Knox. We roomed together in a "bachelor pad" in Louisville and were then assigned to be in the same unit in Erlangen, Germany after the course. We had become great friends and colleagues.

2nd Lieutenant Whelden, Fort Hood, Texas - 1973

So, following the Advanced Course, Bob and I took up Major Montgomery's offer. Stopping to consult your career manager was encouraged by Armor Branch, as it was an opportunity to have face-to-face counseling on your career and assignments. After discussing our respective career paths, he took us to dinner at a restaurant on the top floor of a hotel overlooking the nation's capital. (Eerily, this was the same hotel that I was at on 9/11 while attending an Army conference 24 years later, a story I share in Chapter 16.)

At that time, Tom Montgomery was also a Senior White House Military Social (Protocol) Aide to the President of the United States. This meeting with him in 1977 started a relationship that lasts to this day. He is close enough to my family that my son's middle name is Thomas. I later became his Operations Officer when he was commanding a brigade as a colonel.

During his time in Somalia in 1992, Tom was a two-star general and the Deputy United Nations Force Commander under a three-star Turkish general. He also wore a second hat, commander of U.S. Forces, that made him responsible for the performance and safety of U.S. troops assigned there.

Somalia was a humanitarian disaster, with tens of thousands of civilians starving to death. It was a political morass in the aftermath of a violent civil war. Clan warfare was stalling the humanitarian effort and the UN decided to intervene to ensure that relief could get to the people. Later, the mission became one of nation-building.

The United States joined the humanitarian effort with the best of intentions under President Bush and then supported the expanded mission to bring peace between opposing warlords and rebuild political institutions supported by the new Clinton Administration. But we quickly found the UN force challenged militarily beyond the means to respond in-kind. Because the mission was primarily designed to be a humanitarian assistance effort and the level of violence had been underestimated, U.S. forces were lightly armed and unprepared for any type of significant conflict.

Montgomery realized there was a need for added combat power to protect the force, and in August he sent a request to General Joseph Hoar, the Central Command Commander (his immediate U.S. boss), for tanks and armored vehicles *at the earliest possible date.* He added, *"I believe that U.S. forces are at risk without it."*

He asked for 28 M1 Abrams tanks and 28 Bradley Fighting Vehicles. Hoar's initial reaction to that request during a face-to-face meeting in Mogadishu was: *"This isn't going to fly politically, Tom."* Montgomery replied: *"Yes sir, but it's what I need."* Hoar directed him to reduce the size of the requested force and Montgomery resubmitted a new request on September 14. Hoar passed the reduced request to the Pentagon on the 23 September, but Defense Secretary Les Aspin turned it down. Ten days later, on October 3rd, 18 Americans were killed in a battle that is now widely known as "Black Hawk Down."

Major General Montgomery in Mogadishu - 1992

Montgomery had to scramble to borrow some lightly-armored UN Malaysian vehicles and four old Pakistani tanks to add to his heroic foot-bound infantry battalion, 2-14 Infantry, from the 10th Mountain Division. That joint force, commanded by a great battalion commander, Lieutenant Colonel Bill David, fought all night and took additional casualties (including Malaysians and Pakistanis) before finally reaching and rescuing surrounded Rangers. Aspin subsequently accepted responsibility for disapproving Montgomery's request, and resigned.

Almost exactly 20 years later, a similar situation played out Benghazi, Libya, where we lost Ambassador Chris Stevens and Sean Smith, as well as Tyrone Woods and Glen Doherty; CIA security contractors who responded to the initial attack. At least 10 congressional investigations followed, but what now seems clear is that requests for additional security prior to the attack were denied by state department officials. Ultimately, several senior state department officials resigned and Secretary of State Hillary Clinton accepted responsibility for the security lapses.

> *Military commanders must always tell their civilian bosses and the political leadership what they need to get the job done - without trying to judge what might ultimately be politically acceptable.*

Lessons from these sad episodes are self-evident. Military commanders must always tell their civilian bosses and the political leadership what they need to get the job done – without trying to judge what might ultimately be politically acceptable. Let the civilian and political leadership make that call.

Both of these episodes drew tactical and operational-level lessons, but had strategic implications. A commander must always give his boss his best military advice. And yes, if you put a commander in charge, you should support him, or relieve him if you think he's wrong-minded about the mission. Military professionals make the case and then do the best job possible with what they are given.

Regrettably (and too often), politics does trump military strategy, and the results are all too familiar. We've learned this lesson, and repeated it, far too many times.

Some Personal Experiences with Trust

If you believe everything depends on *you* to ensure it is done properly, then you're in for a rough road ahead. It can be hard to relinquish control, but leaders need to delegate—and to do that, you need to trust those below you… and the people below them… and then the folks below them.

There's no question that an organization's strength and output is only as good as the people in it, but demonstrating trust, and then allowing people to do their job, should be the goal of every new leader. People often perform at their highest level if they know they are trusted. The great writer Ernest Hemingway put it this way, in his inimitable style: "*The best way to find out if you can trust somebody is to trust them.*"

I've often told people in new organizations I joined that I trust them until that trust is violated. This puts a *healthy* kind of pressure on them NOT to violate that trust. Stronger performance is often the result. That is why I say that the job of a leader is to inspire people to be their best. They will often deliver exactly that if they know they are trusted.

Here are two stories that demonstrate the value of trust: one that reflects what happens when there is *no* trust, and another that reflects the tremendous performance and learning that comes when there *is* trust.

When No Trust Exists

This story occurred around 1993. I had just completed attendance at the Army War College in Carlisle, Pennsylvania. This senior-level schooling brings together the best of senior lieutenant colonels and colonels—along with other Services' and foreign officers from around the world—to study the operational and strategic art of war, with a sprinkling of diplomacy so warriors know there are other tools in their tool box besides just lethal means.

During that year, I found out I would return to Germany after graduation. It would be to one of premier jobs for a former lieutenant colonel commander: operations officer for one of the Army's 12 Divisions, three of which were based in Germany. Unfortunately, I learned during our year at Carlisle that one of them, the 8th Infantry Division, would be disbanded—the one I had been selected for. I eventually ended up in Wurzburg, Germany as the operations officer for the 3rd Infantry Division. Major General Rich Keller was the commanding general and hired me sight unseen, mostly on the recommendation of senior officers such as Monty Meigs and Tom Montgomery, both of whom I had worked for previously.

This became the toughest job I ever had, up to that point. Having served two tours in Germany, all in Bavaria, I thought I was familiar with the way things were done. I was in my element, but my plate was overflowing. I had to deal with war planning, major field exercises, and large training events in two separate locations in Germany, as well as the day-to-day operations of the division. I had many 18-hour days, more than a few nights where I just crashed on a couch in the office, and some long stretches "in the field."

The eye-opening experience related to trust that I had during this time was when I led a military-to-military exchange trip to Hungary, one of the satellite countries of the former Soviet Union. The Cold War had ended, and we were now opening the aperture to Eastern European countries that had been coerced into the Warsaw Pact decades earlier by the strong arm of Russia.

After the Berlin Wall fell in 1989, General George Joulwan, the Supreme Allied Commander of all military forces in Europe, established a program called "Partnership for Peace" or PfP. His idea was to conduct military-to-military exchanges, reaching across the former Iron Curtain so new relationships could be forged between the U.S. and its former foes. The goal was to pull the Warsaw Pact nations out of Russia's sphere of influence and into ours.

My trip was the first such effort the U.S. military did with Hungary, and I was able to witness the difference in approaches to trust between the US military and the Eastern European military—and, by extension, the Russians, since Soviet satellite countries' military dogma mirrored the mother ship.

The Hungarians were truly trying to impress us when they showed us their weaponry, but they were seemingly unaware that the decades-old equipment they had was far inferior to ours, if they had to face us in war. The Russians had given frontline nations in Eastern Europe the oldest and least capable equipment, saving the best for themselves. Soviet satellite countries such as Hungary, Czechoslovakia, Poland, and East Germany—that were rolled into the Soviet arc after World War II—were frankly viewed as cannon-fodder by the Russians.

Although I was only a lieutenant colonel at the time, I was treated like a general. Everywhere I turned, only officers (majors and above) were briefing us. They had little trust in their more junior officers and sergeants, like the U.S. places in our junior leaders. Russian influence was everywhere and the lack of trust and regimentation contrasted sharply with the way the U.S. military operates, where mission orders are issued along with the commander's intent, thereby giving subordinates the freedom to operate within that framework. In the U.S. military, it's all about trust and empowerment. I saw little of that in Hungary.

The Hungarians put up me and my team in a lakeside resort reserved for senior military officials. I remember walking into my "dacha" and thinking I had just taken a step back in time. Everything in that cottage was 1950s era—from the lights to the handle on the refrigerator door.

A few months later, we reciprocated by bringing senior military leaders from Hungary to our bases in Germany. Most of these delegations consisted of colonels and generals. They were shocked when we turned them over to our sergeants (who actually gave the briefings) and even more shocked when we let them mingle with our troops—out of our earshot—to see what U.S. soldiers were really like.

General Joulwan's approach obviously worked, as a number of former Soviet Union countries are now members of the North Atlantic Treaty Organization (NATO): the Czech Republic, Poland, Bulgaria, Estonia, Latvia, Lithuania, Romania, Slovakia, Slovenia, Albania, Croatia, and Montenegro.

And yes, Hungary.

When Trust Exists

I eventually found myself on the list for both colonel and command. My boss called me in one day and told me that he had both good and bad news. The good news was that I was now the *"proud owner of a golf course."* The bad news was that I was now the *"proud owner of a golf course."*

He was telling me that I had been selected to command an Army base, rather than what I had spent 20 years preparing for: an armored brigade. In fact, it was the base we were on: the 98th Area Support Group (ASG), headquartered right there in Wurzburg, Germany.

I recall thinking at the time, *"There must be some mistake. I don't know anything about running a base, and, quite frankly, I'm not interested in learning."*

It took me just a few months to realize this turn of events was the best thing that ever happened to me, professionally. I learned more about trusting the people below me than I ever would have had I continued on the traditional Army path.

Over 95 percent of my 3,000-person workforce was civilian, half were females, and an equal number were German nationals. I was like a "town mayor" serving more than 45,000 constituents and customers. My leadership style needed to adapt to this very different environment or I would fail. I was joining THEIR team and needed to learn quickly how to adapt to THEIR environment.

I pulled out my Philosophy of Command (see Appendix A) from my time at Fort Knox and retooled it to target a very different kind of audience. I found that commanding a base—something I had no experience with—required me to put trust, faith, and confidence in a workforce that knew much more about the tasks at hand than I did. I had to lead the team, but at the same time, I had to have confidence that their shared feedback and advice to me was of value.

They needed to know that I trusted them.

The leadership skills I employed at that time had little to do with the technical aspects of running an Army base, but rather, those that required skills at simply leading people; something I had spent 20 years honing. I found myself praising and encouraging what was working well, and just as importantly, I sought to learn for myself what was not working well and how we could make it better. It wasn't difficult sorting out the two, as all I had to do was pay attention to the "constituents" in my community; those on the receiving end of what we provided. Simply put, I listened to my "customers." They could be very vocal when something wasn't right. I understood this well, since I too had been a customer of the community for the previous 18 months.

This experience helped me grow as a leader and prepared me for the rest of my time in uniform and beyond. My career—and my life—were positively shaped by this turn of events. Frankly, I'm not sure I would have seen the success that I experienced thereafter had I not taken this road less traveled—something I didn't initially embrace at the time.

> *It should be intuitive to most leaders that the higher you climb up the corporate ladder, the greater the reliance you must have on those below you.*

Be careful what you wish for.

It should be intuitive to most leaders that the higher you climb up the corporate ladder, the greater the reliance you must have on those below you. Support your team and let them do their job and you'll be amazed at what they give back.

Finally, senior leaders must be an organization's biggest cheerleader. I tell this to newly selected generals, but it also applies to the corporate world. Inspire people to be their best and praise them when they deliver. Foster a climate where people *want* to come to work because of your inspirational leadership. Place trust in them and you will be surprised at the positive returns on that investment.

That's what I tried to do in the 98th ASG, and it worked.

3

Are You My Mentor?

"The greatest good you can do for another is not just
to share your riches but to reveal to him his own."
Benjamin Disraeli

When I met with Major Montgomery in Washington D.C. on my way to Germany in the summer of 1977, I never expected that he would become my first true mentor. There was no contractual agreement or even a discussion about such a relationship, and through all these years, I've never mentioned the word "mentor" to him. But, throughout our relationship, our conversations have given me volumes of knowledge about leadership and a host of other topics.

I saw in him a leadership style similar to my own, just more seasoned. I wanted to learn as much as I could from him and use similar techniques as my own leadership responsibilities grew. He helped me get certain jobs and I worked directly for him once. We remain great friends to this day.

Receiving mentorship is a vital element in learning about leadership… and being a mentor is one of the responsibility of all great leaders.

I believe there are four types of mentors: assigned, self-appointed, sought-after, and what I call "virtual." I have experienced all four. The first three are rather self-evident in terms of what they mean. What I've found the most valuable, however, is this last one, *virtual.*

What do I mean?

Virtual mentorship is something you do on your own. You simply pay attention to all of the people around you and learn from them. This can apply to both your professional and personal life. Pay attention to what others do or say that is particularly smart or good, then adopt it as your own habit. Notice also when a leader does something incredibly dumb or harmful to others, then put that in your leadership reservoir as well, so that you will never do the same. We've all seen good and bad behavior and said to ourselves: *"If I ever get into that position, I hope I behave—or **do not** behave—like that."*

Think of your life as a journey carrying a backpack, and observed behaviors are rocks you find along the path. Pick up both the good and bad—the good for future use and the bad to remind you not to repeat what those rocks represent. I've got plenty of rocks in my backpack—of both kinds—that I've picked up along my life's journey. All great leaders learn something from those they encounter along their journey.

It's also a good practice to acknowledge those who provided meaningful lessons. I regularly cite those who taught me something that I now use myself. I also store away lessons that I want to avoid from leaders who I don't want to emulate, though I generally refrain from naming them.

Perhaps one of the greatest periods during which I learned from others was my time in the Pentagon in the late 1990s. My 23 years of service to that point had been exclusively within Army ranks, with no duty served in another military branch. But in 1996, when I became a new brigadier general, I was assigned to the Joint Staff in the Pentagon.

I served during this time with a number of great military leaders who influenced me. Lieutenant General Pete Pace (later Chairman of the Joint Chiefs of Staff) was the J3 of the Joint Staff. I had to brief him each morning. My immediate supervisor was first Major General John Van Alstyne, then later Rear Admiral Tim Keating (who eventually became the Pacific Command Commander and Northern Command Commander as a 4-star admiral). Brigadier General Jim Conway (later Commandant of the Marine Corps) was a fellow 1-star and Colonel David Petraeus was the Executive Officer for the Chairman of the Joint Chiefs of Staff, General Hugh Shelton.

Lieutenant Colonel Terry "Guts" Robling served there as well, and would later become my boss as a three-star general when he commanded Marine Corps Forces Pacific and I was his civilian Executive Director. That was a particularly interesting relationship, as he was a lieutenant colonel when I was a brigadier general in 1996. While he didn't report to me, we knew each other and occasionally worked together. Seventeen years later, I reported to him.

I remember our first discussion in his office in 2013, where I made clear that while we had a different relationship in the Pentagon, I was perfectly fine working *for* him. I remember him saying he was, as well.

Good leaders don't patent their behavior; they willingly pass it on.

He was very comfortable in his own skin. We got along great in the two years of his command tenure and remain good friends to this day.

Good leaders don't patent their behavior; they willingly pass it on. I have borrowed many leadership techniques—perhaps most of them—from others who freely gave them up, and from some who didn't even know I took them. Let your greatest legacy be that you pass on the best-of-breed leadership traits you've learned from others.

I freely pass on mine. Many are in this book.

4

Delivering Under Pressure

"No Pressure, No Diamonds"
Thomas Carlyle

Serving in Germany in the late 1970s was no picnic. The U.S. had just come off a very unpopular war in Vietnam, transitioned the military to an all-volunteer force, and lowered our recruiting standards to keep the number of new enlistees up. Carter Administration cuts to the defense budget hurt both readiness and modernization, and the lower induction standards brought in some recruits who didn't represent the best of America.

I was assigned to a tank battalion in Erlangen, Germany in 1977, initially as the Assistant Operations Officer, a standard staff job for a newly-minted captain waiting for command of a company. About six months into this job, my boss was fired and I replaced him—but without an assistant to replace the now-vacant position I had just left.

The next few months were a blur of activity. My tank battalion participated in major field exercises, gunnery training, and war planning. Eventually a major came into the battalion to replace me, and I was able to move on to command a tank company—the most coveted job for any Army captain.

My work during this period had both highs and lows. Because of the lower quality of recruits during the late 70s, there were major drug problems across the force, including in Germany. I put my Executive Officer (2nd in command) in Fort Leavenworth's prison for dealing drugs and I discharged a number of soldiers associated with drugs or other misconduct.

*Karen and me just after taking command of
Charlie Company, 1-35 Armor - 1978*

This period was the height of the Cold War with the Soviet Union, so each winter, the U.S. military conducted a major training exercise called Return of Forces to Germany (REFORGER). It was designed to demonstrate to the Soviets that we could quickly mobilize forces and "return" them to Germany in the event of a Soviet invasion into Western Europe. It generally ran two weeks and was conducted across the frozen German landscape, particularly in areas where we actually expected to fight. It included hundreds of units throughout Europe, but the Pentagon also brought over to Europe thousands of military personnel from the United States who utilized pre-stored equipment such as tanks and artillery.

It was just before one of these annual exercises that our brigade received a new commander. Colonel (Col.) John Petracca was a hard, no-nonsense trainer and experienced war fighter who made some people nervous in his presence, with his George Patton-esque persona. Prior to the large winter exercise, Col. Petracca assembled the nine tank company commanders in his brigade to teach us how to evaluate the ability of a tank to cross under-classed bridges. Tanks weigh more than 50 tons and many of the bridges in Germany are marked for lesser weight. This training was an intersection of physics, risk assessment, and safety that most of us didn't fully appreciate prior to his class. But we followed his guidance and prevailed in the exercise without breaking any bridges, damaging any tanks, or injuring any soldiers.

I'll never know whether his techniques for crossing these bridges actually weakened any of them, but having served in Germany for decades afterwards, I've not heard of a single bridge collapse resulting from a tank crossing done the "Petracca-way." And, we were training for war, so knowing what bridges would support tanks and what bridges would not was key to our plans.

Prior to this exercise, Col. Petracca also challenged each and every one of his 30+ company-sized units to take every major piece of equipment into the field and bring it all back under its own power. He told us that any company that accomplished this would receive a four-day weekend and the bragging rights that came with it. A typical company had anywhere from 20-30 vehicles. Mine had 17 tanks and a half dozen other support vehicles.

As it turned out, my company was one of the few to meet this challenge, but that brought more attention my way, which I wasn't sure I really wanted. From that point forward, Col. Petracca gave me and my company more attention than I was looking for. To me, it felt like we became the new standard that he charged others to meet.

A few months after the exercise, I was walking out of my tank park one evening and Col. Petracca's car pulled up. He rolled down his window and said: *"Craig, tomorrow your company is going to be inspected by the Division's MAIT team…and you're going to show everyone how to pass."* MAIT stood for Maintenance Assistance and Inspection Team, and these visits brought with them standards almost nobody could meet. No company in our brigade had passed this inspection in a very long time.

This was considered a "no notice" inspection, given that I had only 12 hours to prepare. It was 6 p.m. now, and at 6 a.m. the following morning, a dozen inspectors would be climbing all over my company's tanks. That was a long night, but we passed the inspection and I can still feel the clap of Col. Petracca's hand on the back of my neck as he stood me in front of 30+ of my fellow company commanders to demonstrate to them that it could be done.

I was proud of my team, but also a bit embarrassed by the adulation. Nevertheless, I learned valuable lessons from Col. Petracca during these months. My confidence rose that day as I came to understand that delivering under pressure is what distinguishes great leaders from, well, so-so leaders.

I learned another lesson about delivering results in another REFORGER exercise a year or so later. My company had just implemented the tank crossing technique taught to us by Col. Petracca: to surreptitiously make our way through "the enemy's defenses" and get behind their front lines, where we could wreak havoc in their rear area. I was very proud of my team that day, but an observing General Officer from the U.S. mainland zeroed in on the fact that some of my soldiers did not have the right uniform on, and our tank tarps were flapping in the wind as they went by. He reported his observation of this "sloppy-looking" tank company, which eventually found its way back to me. No mention was made of our tactical success.

This was an example of what I later dubbed "Be Good, Look Good" – an approach I incorporated into my philosophy of command (see Appendix A) regarding pride in one's work and the work environment. It reminds me of the uniform standards General Patton demanded of his troops even in combat during World War II. A clean and orderly work environment raises pride and a sense of ownership by the people who work there. Whether in a military environment or in the corporate world, people perform better when they, and their work environment, are held to high standards of appearance and organization.

> *A clean and orderly work environment raises pride and a sense of ownership by the people who work there.*

First impressions actually do count, I learned.

The risk for leaders is to ensure that you aren't covering up rust with paint, or making work for work's sake. I've seen that phenomenon, and it is counter-productive. You must create a culture in which people take pride in their work, their environment, and themselves. The organization will be better off as a result. Believe me.

In my career, I have encountered many leaders who taught me the value of having pride in one's work. Key among these was Col. Petracca. Though initially unnerved by his style of leadership, I ultimately became inspired by him and learned over time what he was doing and why.

Throughout my time as a company commander, he often tested and evaluated me as a leader. Once he sought me out during a major field exercise at Hohenfels Training Area and got into my tank when I crossed the line of departure on a simulated night-time attack. For the next 5-6 hours, he was just two feet away in the loader's hatch—never saying much, just observing and listening to how I commanded my company. When we arrived on the objective near dawn the next morning, he disembarked, simply saying, *"Have a great day."*

In the field with my tank company – 1979

For all the angst this senior-level commander created among junior officers, he was a demanding but fair taskmaster and leader. Those who understood this succeeded. Those who shrank from it did not. While his leadership style was different from my own, it worked, and I truly appreciate the time I had him as a mentor and commander. He was a true warrior, a very capable leader, and a fine man. Sadly, I learned that a few years after his retirement from the Army, he was killed in a hunting accident, but the legacy of and lessons learned from his leadership have carried with me to this day.

5

Effective Communications

"It's not what we say that matters...
it's what the other person hears."

Author Unknown

I n the summer of 1980, after three years in Germany, I moved to Washington D.C. It was the start of the Reagan years, with a resurgence in national pride in the American military. I was an "Assignment Officer" in the Armor Branch, responsible for the professional development and assignment of junior Armor officers across the globe—the same job Tom Montgomery had when I met him three years earlier. This gave me exposure to the personnel files of my contemporaries, and I was charged with making decisions on assignments that would, first and foremost, fulfill Army requirements, but could also help or hinder their career paths.

The conundrum facing assignment officers like me was that we had to be mindful of a key principle: *Army requirements are a higher priority than the (personal) professional development of the Officer Corps.* We had to accept that not everyone could have a career-enhancing posting. This made for difficult decisions, as I felt a great responsibility to choose the right officers for each assignment, while also never taking into account personal relationships. I was also very aware that following my duty in Washington, I would be returning to the field to serve with many of the same officers for whom I had made career-impacting decisions. I was committed to be fair and honest with each and every one of them so they knew I did my best on both counts. I had to ensure I could look myself in the mirror every day, and that years later, I could also look them in the eye and feel that same confidence.

It was during this tour, communicating to Armor officers all over the world, that I started to be more aware of everything I said or wrote. This is where I started to hone the skill of "connecting to my audience." I learned that a key to effective communication is understanding—before you transmit—how your audience will **receive** your message.

If you first figure out how to best connect to OTHERS in terms THEY best understand, you have the greatest chance of success.

Whether engaging a single individual or an audience of a thousand, it is essential to connect to them in terms they best understand. It doesn't matter if it is a 20- or a 60-year-old; a male or female; a private or general; an American or a foreigner; a liberal or a conservative; a CEO or a line worker. If you first figure out how to best connect to OTHERS in terms THEY best understand, you have the greatest chance of success.

I now analyze my audiences and have practiced this technique for years. When I'm invited to speak to a group, and preparation time allows for it, I study my audience in depth. For example, in a recent six-year period, I was a "Senior Mentor" for a Department of Defense course called the "Executive Leader Development Program." In this role, I traveled once a year as part of a group of highly motivated, smart, and ambitious Department of Defense civilians and military members. I would spend a week in far-flung locations with them, mentoring and advising both small groups and individuals.

At the beginning of each trip, I would give a talk called *A Potpourri of Thoughts on Leadership and Other Stuff.* I studied the students' biographies ahead of time to find any connections I might have with them. I then selected half a dozen of them and placed their names randomly among the slides I was showing during my talk. Whenever a slide came up with someone's name on it, I would ask them to stand and I would convey to the group what we had in common. (I would announce this up front, so the students would not be surprised.)

This accomplished two things: it obviously kept the audience awake during my presentation—anxious to see if their name was on a slide— but more importantly, it allowed me to connect with them in a more personal way, demonstrating that I cared enough to study them ahead of time. Understanding your audience, then communicating to them in terms they best understand, is an essential skill of an effective leader. Without it, the leadership mountain is a much steeper climb.

Knowing your audience is especially important in *written* communications when body language, facial expression, tone, and verbal inflections and intensity cannot be observed. Whenever writing, it's best to start with a first draft—what General Stan McChrystal calls the "30 percent solution"—because there's another 70 percent of fine-tuning still to be done. If time allows, let your draft sit a few hours, then return to it and self-edit your writing, improving it as much as you can. It always gets better when you reread your work and do further editing.

Any time that you have a strong emotion associated with your written message, it's best to let it sit overnight, before pushing "send." Come back to it later—when the drama is less—as this will give you the opportunity to repackage it in a way that will usually be better received, while not diluting the impact of your original intent.

Years ago, *"Read back for possible correction"* was a critical refrain on tactical radios in the military. This referred to having the receiver repeat the message to ensure it was fully understood and there would be no confusion over a radio. I continue to follow this rule when it comes to any communicating I do. Time permitting, it's helpful to "read back" *to myself* what I intend to say—whether verbally or in writing—before doing so.

This is a case where patience pays.

6

Know Your Working Style... and Those Around You

*In the progress of personality, first comes
a declaration of independence, then a
recognition of interdependence.*

Henry Van Dyke

W hen people speak of diversity, they are usually referring to race, gender, ethnicity, age, and sometimes nationality. All are important, but there's another form of diversity that I suggest leaders pay attention to: personality type. People vary extensively in their personality types, and having such diversity in an organization or on a team usually pays off with better results.

There are numerous tests to assess personality type, but I have come to appreciate and use the well-known and generally accepted Myers-Briggs Type Indicator (MBTI). I first took the MBTI when I was a student at Fort Leavenworth attending the Army's Command and General Staff College (CGSC)—a graduate-level professional development training course for majors. Established in 1881 by General William

Tecumseh Sherman, the institution was initially the *School of Application for Infantry and Cavalry*. The historic Army post sits on the bluffs of the Missouri River, just north of Kansas City. One of the great benefits of this one-year academic sabbatical is the opportunity to spend time with 800 contemporaries and learn from them. These are the leaders of tomorrow's Army. Relationships forged there endure for decades. While I was in this program, I was also earning a master's degree at night in Kansas City, so this year truly tested my commitment to improving myself.

> *Having diverse personality types can make a team exponentially more effective, by drawing the very best skills out of each and every member to benefit the whole.*

The MBTI is often used in both the federal government and in the business sector to help people identify the nature of their own personality type and accompanying strengths and weaknesses. It also helps one to understand *other people's* personalities as well, so as a leader, you can maximize *their* strengths and mitigate *their* weaknesses. Whether in the military or in the corporate world, it is the strength of the whole that pushes organizations to their best results. Having diverse personality types can make a team exponentially more effective, by drawing the very best skills out of each and every member to benefit the whole.

I've taken the MBTI half a dozen times over the years and it always shows that I am an "ISTJ" (Introversion, Sensing, Thinking, and Judgment). My personality type is generally described as:

- Serious and quiet, earns success by concentration and thoroughness;
- Practical, orderly, matter-of-fact, logical, realistic, and dependable;
- Takes responsibility;

- Make up his own mind as to what should be accomplished and works toward it steadily, regardless of protest or distraction.

Myers-Briggs has 16 different profiles with different combinations of personality traits. For example, the opposite of Introversion (I) is Extroversion (E). The opposite of Sensors (S) is Intuitive (N). The opposite of Thinkers (T) are Feelers (F) and the opposite of Judgers (J) are Perceivers (P). You can see how these can be mixed and matched to arrive at 16 different combinations.

Further, there are ranges or degrees of each type. For example, you can be at the far end of the spectrum for introversion, or closer to the middle, where you might show extroversion in some instances. I happen to be at the far end of introversion, but the other components of my profile—the S, T, and J—give me the ability to be "extroverted" when a particular task calls for it, like public speaking: a skill not normally associated with an introvert.

A friend once told me he was one of five company commanders in a particular unit, and his boss didn't understand why he was not connecting well with his junior leaders. He made them all take a Myers-Briggs test and he learned that they were all extroverts, while he was an introvert. From that point on, communications improved because they better understood each other and he took their personality differences into account when he communicated with them.

Understanding the nature of different personalities on your team is one of the rocks you need in your leadership backpack. It would be a boring world if everyone thought and acted the same, as well as a less productive and less innovative one. There is strength in diverse personalities, just as there are strengths in other forms of diversity.

Do you know your profile? Have you ever had an assessment to better understand your own personality style? What about the styles of those around you? Your performance as a leader will improve if you know more about the operating style of the people you lead. Check it out. You can take the test in 30 minutes online at www.mbtionline.com.

Generational Diversity

Finally, it is equally important to understand distinctions between *generational* groups: starting with *Baby Boomers* (born between the early-to-mid 1940s and ending between 1960 – 1964). Members of this large post-World War II group are now becoming senior citizens. (I know because I'm one of them and I'm starting to feel my age.)

The next group is *Generation X*, born between the early-to-mid 1960s and the early 1980s. Following them are *Millennials*, typically born in a window between the early 80s and the mid-90s to early 2000s. (Research indicates that this group will have 73 million members by 2019, surpassing the *Baby Boomers* in size). *Generation Z*, also called the *post-Millennials, Homeland Generation*, or *Plurals* is the cohort of people who followed the *Millennials*, born between the mid-1990s to the mid-2000s.

All were shaped by both the environment in which they were raised and by the nurture and influence (or lack of) by parents, educators, coaches and peers. Because these factors evolved so substantially over the 50-60-year period in question, there are great variations in outcomes regarding how each group thinks, acts, conducts themselves, the depth of their work ethic, and their expectations from society and of themselves. Too much for this book to undertake, a good primer on better understanding generational differences is *"The Generational Imperative"* by Chuck Underwood.

And, because leaders often find themselves leading people with both personality *and* generational differences, it argues for the strong leader to study both.

I can assure you the military is doing so, and the corporate world would be wise to do so as well.

7

Loyalty is a Two-way Street

*"If I have seen further, it is by standing
on the shoulders of giants."*

Sir Isaac Newton

In the summer of 1987, I became the Chief of Cavalry Doctrine at Fort Knox, responsible for writing and revising all the training and doctrinal manuals for the Armored Cavalry forces of the Army. This is when I first met Lieutenant Colonel Jerry Wallace Thurman, better known as "J.W." He was my immediate boss and a legend in Armor branch.

Having earned the Distinguished Service Cross for bravery—one level below the Medal of Honor—as a helicopter pilot in Vietnam, he was cut from the same cloth as a character from the 1979 movie *Apocalypse Now*, the irreverent story about the Vietnam War starring Martin Sheen and Robert Duvall as Lt. Col Bill Kilgore, the eccentric cavalryman. J.W. was Kilgore, the bare-chested, stetson-wearing commander who surfed behind a patrol boat on the Mekong Delta River.

Never politically correct, his was a unique style of leadership; one that would be difficult for me to replicate, but I carry some of his

One of his most endearing qualities was an intense loyalty to his troops.

leadership rocks in my backpack. One of his most endearing qualities was an intense loyalty to his troops.

J.W. retired as a colonel and stayed at Fort Knox, where he spent a number of years mentoring tomorrow's Armor and Cavalry leaders. Regrettably, he passed away a few years ago, but his legacy—and particularly the fervent loyalty to the thousands of soldiers he touched—survived and has made us all better for it.

I first met J.W.'s younger brother, Major James David Thurman, during this tour. He is known as "J.D." and was at Fort Hood, Texas when I was at Fort Knox working for his older brother. He too was an Armor and Cavalry officer, and like his brother, a pilot. J.D. and I would serve together a few years later in Germany and became good friends. He rose to become the commander of all forces in Korea when he retired as a four-star general in 2013.

Ironically, my adopting of J.W.'s commitment to loyalty to his team was tested later in my career. In November of 2009, the Marine Corps announced the creation of a new Senior Executive Service (SES) position in Hawaii to oversee bases and stations in the Pacific, and the move of thousands of Marines from Okinawa to Guam and other locations. I was living in Florida at the time, but my wife and I were anxious to return to Hawaii, so I applied for the job.

About mid-January of 2010, I received a phone call from the Marine Corps; they asked if I could come to Quantico, Virginia for an interview near the end of the month. I went and was interviewed by two Marine Corps brigadier generals and a member of the Senior Executive Service. Twenty minutes before the interview, I was provided a list of questions I was told they would ask. This wasn't expected, but I appreciated the opportunity to wrap my head around the questions and formulate a response to each.

When I went in, they dutifully asked each of the questions and I responded, but once done with the questions on the list, one of them asked: *"What would you say to the selecting official if you had him alone for 30 seconds in an elevator?"* I responded that I would not repeat what was already in my application since I would assume he had already reviewed it. I said: *"I would invite him to speak to anyone who I have <u>worked for</u>, has worked <u>with me</u>, or has worked <u>for me</u>. They all will say the same thing about Craig Whelden."*

I wanted to assure these board members that they would find no one who would characterize me as treating superiors one way and subordinates another. I have worked for people like that and it was never pleasant. I was confident enough in the answer to this question that I was happy to put this challenge out to them.

I returned to Florida and a few days later, I received a call from Hawaii. They asked if I could do a telephone interview on 7 February with Lieutenant General Keith Stalder, the commander of U.S. Marine Corps Forces Pacific. I said I certainly could, but by coincidence, I would be arriving in Hawaii on 6 February on a two-week vacation visiting my son, who was a college student there. I said I'd be happy to meet with him face-to-face. Surprised to hear this, they said they'd get back to me the following day.

When I hung up, my spirits were up. I had apparently done well enough in the panel interview that I was now at the next level of the application. The next day, the phone rang and it was the same person. *"No,"* he said, *"a telephone interview is all that's needed."* As I hung up, I turned to my wife and told her that I didn't believe I had gotten the job. *"Why in the world would they not take advantage of a face-to-face interview?"* I asked myself. I later learned that the organization was trying to set the same conditions for all of the final candidates and since others would not have a face-to-face interview, neither should I.

As planned, my wife and I flew to Hawaii on 6 February 2010. The morning after our arrival, I received a call from General Stalder. He didn't inquire about my job qualifications and, in fact, joked about the fact that he wasn't sure what to ask since he had never hired an SES before. I told him that was OK, because I had never been an SES before, so I probably didn't know the answers anyway. He laughed.

Our conversation was really just a chemistry check. At the end of the interview, he asked me if I wanted to leave anything with him. I told him the panel had asked what I would say to him if we found ourselves in an elevator together, and then told him my answer. He laughed again and said the board members had passed that on to him.

Almost two months went by and I didn't hear anything. I was sure I hadn't been selected. Finally, the phone rang on April 1st and I was informed that I had been "tentatively" selected. *"What does that mean?"* I asked. The fellow on the other end of the line said there were three more gates I'd have to get through: concurrence from the Assistant Commandant of the Marine Corps, approval from the Undersecretary of the Navy, and validation from a Board of Senior Executives that I was qualified to serve in their ranks. He told me to not worry. Most of these should be easy, as the first two would likely accept the recommendation of General Stalder, and I should "breeze through" the board review, since I had already served seven years as an active duty General Officer.

Finally, in early May, I was notified that I had been officially selected, and I could negotiate a report date with Marine Corps Forces Pacific. In the end, I'm confident my loyalty both up and down the chain of command paid off.

My point is simply that loyalty is a two-way street.

Bi-polar leadership is toxic and destructive and should be uncovered early on. This is one reason why more and more organizations are now doing 360-degree evaluations—including the military—to ensure they know what they're getting in a senior leader.

It doesn't matter if you are dealing with

Bi-polar leadership is toxic and destructive and should be uncovered early on.

people higher up the command chain or those lower than you—everyone should be treated with respect, dignity, and appreciation for what they do. You've probably heard that saying, *"What you see is what you get."*

In my case, that was (and remains) true, and I value it in others as well.

Setting Organizational Expectations

"High achievement always takes place in the framework of high expectation."
Charles F. Kettering

I was at Fort Knox, Kentucky in 1989, when I was promoted to lieutenant colonel and took command of 2nd Battalion, 10th Cavalry in the 194th Separate Armor Brigade, the largest brigade in the Army. The 194th was part of the 18th Airborne Corps. Also part of the 18th Airborne Corps were the 82nd Airborne Division, based at Fort Bragg, North Carolina; the 101st Air Assault Division, at Fort Campbell, Kentucky; and the 24th Infantry Division at Fort Stewart, Georgia.

We were the Corps' heavy "ready brigade," meaning we were subject to short notification and deployment if called up. I took the flag of command in July 1989 and that very same day, Command Sergeant Major Jerry Utterback joined me as my senior enlisted advisor and command team partner.

After the change of command, we sat down for our first meeting and I told the sergeant major that this relationship was relatively new to me. I had served with command sergeants major before, but had never had one reporting directly to me. He said: *"Sir, that's fine. I've never been a sergeant major before. We'll go on this journey and learn together."* I laughed, as it was clear we would get along great. In retrospect, it now reminds me of the phone interview I had with General Stalder, discussed in the last chapter.

Chemistry counts when you're a senior leader.

Chemistry counts when you're a senior leader.

Jerry Utterback was with me to the end of my command two years later, and eventually became the command sergeant major for the Armor School before retiring. He was a great soldier and we remain close to this day.

I was also blessed to have another great enlisted leader in my ranks during those years. Command Sergeant Major Jack Tilley was our Brigade Sergeant Major. Sergeant Major Tilley rose to become the senior enlisted soldier in our Army: Sergeant Major of the Army.

Both these great soldiers validated for me what I already knew: the key role non-commissioned officers (sergeants) play in making the United States military the best in the world—because officers plan and decide, and sergeants implement and supervise. The key difference between us and much of the rest of the world is that our officers place enormous trust and faith in their non-commissioned officers (NCOs)... *because they've earned it.*

As a leader, I knew that my instructions were being carried out, and when things didn't work out as planned, sergeants adapted because they understood the commander's original intent and goals. That's not the case with many other militaries around the world, I've learned, and that's what sets us apart. I addressed this in Chapter 2, when contrasting the Hungarian Army with the U.S. Army in the early 90s.

Being Upfront About Your Expectations

In the military, newly appointed commanders at the battalion or squadron level and above assume responsibility for an organization of at least 500, but often in the thousands. They typically remain in charge for two years or maybe three, but no more. It's their job to set the course and then lead while they are stewards of the ship.

Occasionally, I've had a new boss who didn't tell us what he thought was important, what his priorities were, or what his personal quirks were. This leads to frustration and the staff and subordinate units often struggled—sometimes for months—trying to figure out exactly what he really wanted. I suggest that a leader's job in business is similar. A boss needs to set expectations, explain a vision, guide the development of a plan, then oversee its execution. He also needs to school his organization on how he operates as a leader so there are few surprises.

To ensure I didn't make this mistake before I took command of the 10th Cavalry, I sat down at my kitchen table with a pen and a yellow legal pad (this was prior to having a personal computer in every household) and I wrote out my "Philosophy of Command" (see Appendix A). I wanted to ensure that from the first day, my soldiers understood what I believed to be important, what was less consequential, and what was non-negotiable.

Written 30 years ago, the foundational principles outlined in this document guide my thinking to this day. Here's the last paragraph:

> *Finally, unit identity is very important to me. I am very proud to be a soldier and am honored to be your commander. This is our battalion, not mine; I have only been given stewardship for the next two years. My regimental affiliation is the 10th Cavalry and there is nowhere I would rather be. I look forward to a very challenging and*

rewarding two years. I'll do my best to make sure they are the same for you.

A few years later, I took charge of a very different type of organization; this time in Germany. I was now a colonel and was selected to command a base spread over seven different communities that supported over 45,000 military, family members, and other "constituents."

I discussed in Chapter 2 how I learned to trust my 3,000 employees. Because my command was made up of mostly civilians of mixed gender (not just men this time), and half were German nationals, I found a need to communicate to this very different work force in a different way, but still I needed to tell them what I thought was important and how I operated.

Again, I wrote down what I wanted to achieve. Like my Philosophy of Command written years before, this document aimed to let this new organization know what I thought was critical in our work versus what was less consequential.

> *I was comfortable enough in my own skin to point out on one of the slides what I thought were my strengths and my weaknesses.*

I also developed a short slide presentation to introduce myself, which I called *Whelden on Whelden* (see Appendix B), to tell them a bit about me so they wouldn't spend months trying to figure out what I thought was important versus not so important. I was comfortable enough in my own skin to point out on one of the slides what I thought were my strengths *and* my weaknesses. On one of the slides, two of the points I made were: *"I follow the rules"* and *"I tend to show all my cards."* Depending on whom you talk to, these can be viewed as either a strength or a weakness, but I wanted everyone to know upfront how I viewed things.

As a new leader, I suggest you not wait for people to figure out what makes you tick. Tell them early, and often, what's important. Give them your vision, set a course, oversee implementation, and lead. If you have a pet peeve, let everyone know so there are no surprises.

Tell them how you operate.

I once worked for a boss whose staff meetings were regularly held at 9 a.m. On the first such meeting, he showed up at about 8:55 and just sat at the end of the long table, saying nothing. A few staff members were already there and others straggled in, but at precisely 9 a.m., he told someone to "lock the door." Two staff officers had not come into the room. In so doing, he made his point. Those officers learned the hard way that "timeliness" was important to him (though I wonder if there wasn't a better way for him to make this point).

Finally, have you ever worked for someone who tries to change the organization right at the outset to shape it to fit their mold? I'm reminded of a quote often attributed to a Roman general from over 2,000 years ago:

> *"We had trained well, but it seemed that every time we were beginning to form up into teams, we reorganized. I was to learn later in life that we tend to meet any new situation by reorganizing... and a wonderful method it can be for creating the illusion of progress while producing confusion, inefficiency, and demoralizing the troops."*

New leaders shouldn't make changes for change's sake right out of the chute. Unless you've been given a mandate for change—or organizational dysfunction is obvious—assume the organization is working well and join *their* team. After an initial assessment period of perhaps 60-90 days, change is then fair game. After all, you are the leader and you are responsible for the ultimate success of those being led. Changing things at the very outset can often be viewed by the organization as a lack of trust or that you think it's dysfunctional or broken.

The Importance of Delegating

Lieutenant colonel command is typically the first time an officer has a large enough organization to warrant a staff. Delegation and time management become even more important. The more senior you become, the broader the responsibilities and organizational span of control you have. Yet, there's still only 24 hours in a day. How do you keep everything moving forward?

In a word, delegate.

An excellent article from the November-December 1999 issue of the Harvard Business Review entitled *"**Management Time: Who's Got the Monkey?**"* (found on the web) relates the story of a leader who organizes his time to the minute. He makes lists; sharpens and lines up his pencils; and gets to the bottom of his inbox before the end of every day. (Sounds like an ISTJ to me.)

Mid-week, one of his subordinates comes in with a difficult problem and asks the leader for help. Because the leader is busy, he tells him to *"send me a memo on that."* He then adds that task to his now-growing list of things to do. This happens three more times before the end of the week, and on Friday, his inbox is overflowing.

Frustrated that he's off his carefully-managed schedule and anxious to get it back on track, he decides to go home Friday night, spend quality time with his family, and return Saturday to catch up. The next day, he drives back to work, passing a local golf course. Turning his head slightly, he sees his four subordinates on the first tee box, getting ready to play a round.

What happened?

When the four subordinates came into his office the previous week, they shifted the "monkeys" on their back to the leader's back.

When subordinates come to me with a problem that I believe they can (and should) solve, I'm happy to provide input, but I make it clear that they *own* the monkey. If they need help, I'm there, but I'm not the action officer.

In the military, there is a process called the Military Decision-Making Process, or MDMP. This seven-step process can work in the corporate world or in everyday life. It includes:

1. Receipt (or issuance) of a mission
2. Analysis
3. Course of action (COA) development
4. COA analysis (aka *wargaming*)
5. COA comparison
6. COA approval
7. Orders production, dissemination, and transition

Typically, a leader is most engaged at steps 1 and 6. What the four subordinates in the Harvard Business Review article did was bring their issues back to the leader at step 2.

With 30 years in an Army uniform, and another nine as a Senior Executive with the Marine Corps, I understand this process well and have used it many times… for even simple decisions at home. It is perfectly adaptable to the corporate world, as well. Done enough times, it becomes like "muscle memory" and is easily incorporated into your daily decision-making.

I can assure you that it will give back perhaps the most important resource you have as a senior leader: **time.**

9

Breaking Down Cultural Barriers

*"You cannot exaggerate about the Marines. They
are convinced to the point of arrogance that they
are the most ferocious fighters on earth – and
the amusing thing about it is that they are."*
Father Kevin Kearney,
1ˢᵗ Marine Division Chaplain, Korean War

E very organization has its own unique culture, derived from explicit and implicit rules about how to behave, talk to others, and get things done. When you are new to an organization, it can be difficult to understand and appreciate this new culture, how it works, and how you fit in.

Adapting to a new culture is a process many leaders will face when they change jobs or find themselves leading an organization whose culture differs from where they came from. I addressed this in the previous chapter when I was selected to command a base after having spent almost 20 years in tank and cavalry units. I've also had the unique opportunity to adapt from one service culture to another: from the Army to the Marine Corps.

In 2010, I became the Executive Director of Marine Corps Forces Pacific, a job I held for more than nine years. I was the senior civilian marine between the Mississippi River and Korea. While some responsibilities were similar to what I had done in the Army, working in the Marine Corps required some adaptation. I was in the same church, but in a different pew. A *very* different pew.

> *Working in the Marine Corps required some adaptation. I was in the same church, but in a different pew. A very different pew.*

The position was created to provide executive level oversight of an $8.7 billion program to build a new base in Guam—the largest such action for the Marine Corps since World War II. The job was framed around management of the bases in the Pacific, but with a special focus on facilitating the move of over 8,500 Marines and 9,000 family members from Okinawa to Guam. I applied for the job, was hired, and started in June 2010. It was a new position, so there was no continuity file of previous work to go by, and the expectations were not completely clear to me at the beginning.

Meeting with my new boss, Lieutenant General Stalder, on my second day at Camp Smith in Hawaii, I told him I understood the job had a lot to do with the building of the new base in Guam and the move of the marines from Okinawa. He confirmed this and mentioned that if he had it his way, the position would have been located in Guam. I replied that if it was based out of Guam, I wouldn't have even known about it, as my job search had only looked for opportunities in Hawaii.

Nevertheless, it was clear I would spend quite a bit of time in Guam; something I hadn't expected when I lifted off from Won Pat International airport in 2003 thinking that would be the last time I would ever visit that small island. I've now lost count of the number of times I've been to Guam. I've also spent a considerable amount of time just north of Guam in the Commonwealth of Northern Mariana Islands. As you'll learn later in the book, the Department of Defense leased two-thirds of the island of Tinian in the early 80s and is now studying the placement of live fire training ranges there. I've been to Tinian over a dozen times in recent years.

After a settling in period, I started to get comfortable with my job, but not so much with the Marine Corps. My sense was that the Marine Corps, in general, did not easily accept outsiders right away. The fact that I was a retired (Army) general meant little to the rank and file. I had to prove my value if I was to move more freely in their ranks. I had to demonstrate that I was worthy of breathing their air. I was fine with that, but it took some time.

The fact is that the Marine Corps thinks they're special... and they are. From the day they first step off a bus whether at Paris Island, South Carolina or at Marine Corps Recruit Depot in San Diego, California, and place their feet in the yellow footprints painted on the concrete, drill instructors start a complete makeover of a recruit to mold them into a marine. It's a special journey culminating in a field exercise affectionately called "the Crucible," where the marines pass their final field test and are presented—in the mud—with the prized Eagle, Globe, and Anchor.

Only then are they a United States Marine.

I ran into General Marty Dempsey in Guam a few years into the job. At the time, he was the Chairman of the Joint Chiefs of Staff, the senior military officer in the United States. We had been contemporaries once, entering the Army about the same time and serving in the same branch (Armor). While we never served together, we knew of each other. He asked me, *"How do you like the Marine Corps?"*

"I love it," I said.

Curious, he asked me to explain. I replied: *"You can find every Marine along a continuum between pride and arrogance, but they'll all be there. We have what we consider 'elite' units in the Army. The Marine Corps is an 'elite'* **Service.***"*

I recently saw a poster that read:

Question: *How long does it take the average person to become a U.S. Marine?*

Answer: *An average person will NEVER be a U.S. Marine.*

I believe that's absolutely true. In my view, the Marine Corps instills a sense of purpose better than any other military service. Marines view themselves, rightly so, as the nation's *"911 Force."* They are ready to go anywhere, at any time, to do anything the nation asks. The motto of Marine Corps Forces Pacific is: *"In Any Clime and Place,"* and you often hear the refrain *"fight tonight."*

That's why there is *"no better friend, no worse enemy, than a U.S. marine"* – a quote attributed to General James Mattis on the eve of Operation Iraqi Freedom when he commanded the 1st Marine Division.

About six or seven months into my job, I found myself "watching paint dry" too often. Working mostly at the operational and strategic level (the reason I was hired), I didn't have enough to do. The build-out of the base in Guam was initially advertised to be completed by 2014, but this was a pipe dream. There was no way a multi-billion-dollar project could be completed that soon. Ultimately, we realized this effort would take 10-15 years at the pace and resourcing stream we were told to expect.

I went to my boss, then Lieutenant General Duane "Drano" Thiessen, and told him I could do more. I could help take some things off his plate; things that were not necessarily in my current job description. I asked him to let me speak to the staff and I would get back to him.

I then called in each staff principal, then their deputies (a civilian GS15 or colonel-equivalent), and told them that I had served in a senior position with the Army here in the Pacific and I understood what this level required. While most of them didn't work directly for me, I was happy to help them whenever and however they needed it. All they had to do was come see me, wind me up, point me in the right direction, and I'd do whatever I could to help facilitate their needs, without adding another layer of bureaucracy to the process.

Different staff sections took advantage of this invitation and soon I had broadened my portfolio beyond just moving Marines from Okinawa to Guam. The extra work helped fill my days and brought me closer to being accepted as a "civilian marine"—one of them.

Since the Marine Corps is part of the broader Department of the Navy, I'm also closer to my Navy brethren in this job than I ever was when I served in an Army uniform. People poke fun every now and then at my Army roots, but it's all in good fun. I'm now officially agnostic each year when Army plays Navy in perhaps the greatest college football rivalry anywhere.

One thing I've learned from the Marine Corps is that—after having served side-by-side with soldiers over the past 18 years in places like Iraq, Afghanistan, and other hot spots around the world—there's a mutual respect for each other that transcends service culture. The respect goes both ways. When you experience adversity together, it brings you together.

I'm proud, honored, and humbled to have been associated with **both** Services *and* **both** cultures.

10

How Tall is Your Ladder?

Be realistic in your expectations.
I'd really like to cuddle a unicorn,
but it ain't going to happen.

India Knight

Before I left mid-level schooling at Fort Leavenworth, Kansas, General Edward "Shy" Meyer, the Chief of Staff of the Army, came to visit our class—as was the habit of every Chief. He was the "CEO" of the Army. We all crowded into what we called the "big blue bedroom"—an auditorium with blue seats—to hear his pitch. After the presentation, he took questions. A major raised his hand and asked: *"Sir, how do you define success in today's Army?"*

General Meyer thought for a moment then replied:

> *"...A career in the Army is like climbing a ladder. When you stand at the bottom and look up, there are many rungs and you may not even see the top. As you reach out to the first rung, your feet are still on the ground and the next rung is within easy reach. As you climb, however, the rungs*

are further apart, the air is thinner, and you start to tire. You'll find that the higher you go, the harder it is to get to the next rung."

He said we all probably thought HE had had a successful career. After all, he was a four-star general and the Chief of Staff of the Army. We all thought *"duh..."*

He then said he had contemporaries who—were they in **his** position—would be disappointed if they retired as *only* the Army Chief of Staff. He paused for the anticipated and confused reaction, which he got from all of us. He then came back to the ladder analogy and made the point that, even for him, there was still another rung on the ladder—the position of Chairman of the Joint Chiefs of Staff. Some of his contemporaries might think it was within reach for him, yet he knew it wasn't.

> *Constantly striving to always reach the next rung is not only unhealthy; it can be at some point impossible and could result in long-held bitterness.*

His point was that everyone needs to aspire to reach an *achievable* rung on the ladder, but we should be satisfied once we arrive there. Constantly striving to always reach the next rung is not only unhealthy; it can be at some point impossible and could result in long-held bitterness.

Following his advice, I told myself that day, *"Self... I want to be a battalion commander."* I had several more rungs on my ladder, but once I reached my goal, I promised myself that I would keep in mind that any new achievement after that would be icing on the cake. I would do my best to excel as a battalion commander, and—though I would continue to be ambitious—I would not *expect* to be promoted to a higher rank.

We all have a "last rung on the ladder," and for most of us, it is somewhere in the middle, not at the top. Aspire to reach a lofty goal, and be satisfied when you arrive. I've spoken to a few colonels over the years who thought they should have been generals, but weren't selected.

Some left the military bitter because they didn't get to that "next rung on their ladder." Some carried this bitterness for years and I could see the toll it took on them. They just couldn't let it go. I've tried to encourage them to reflect on the tremendous career they had up to that point and to look forward to the many great opportunities still ahead.

Then I tell them, "Find a new ladder to climb."

11

The One Percent Advantage

"Life isn't about finding yourself,
it's about creating yourself"
George Bernard Shaw

After the last chapter, cynics might accuse me of suggesting you set a low bar and be satisfied once you get there. This chapter aims to clarify my point further and encourage you to be the best that you can be in whatever you do.

Always.

It's about setting *realistic* expectations and then NOT being *dissatisfied* if you don't get to the next rung on the ladder after you reach your *original* goal.

But because most of you are likely Type A high achievers, I'd like to focus in this chapter on what separates the good from great... and the great from the REALLY great... citing a 2017 article by James Clear: *The 1 Percent Rule: Why a Few People Get Most of the Rewards.* You can find this article on his website.

In his article, Clear describes a 19th century Italian named Pareto who becomes curious about why just a few pea pods in his garden produced most of the peas. He was a mathematician and happened to be also studying why the wealthy seem to have an easier time of becoming even wealthier. He discovered that in Italy, 80% of the land was owned by just 20% of the people; and in England, 70% of the total income was earned by 30% of Brits.

This idea that most of the rewards go to a small group was found to be valid across a number of areas. Pareto published a theory in the early 20th century that has come to be known as the *Pareto Principle* or more commonly, the 80/20 rule. If you apply the *Pareto Principle* to today, this phenomenon is born out in a number of ways.

Why do the rich get richer? For most of us, we're taught at an early age the "miracle of compounding" when we begin investing. Simply put, $10,000 hidden under a mattress or buried in the ground for 30 years will still be only $10,000 (actually less, when you consider inflation). But if the $10,000 is invested at 7% interest over a 30-year period, and compounded monthly, it will be worth over $81,000. This is why rich people don't hide money under their mattress.

You shouldn't, either.

Why do athletes get million-dollar endorsement contracts for doing little more than lending their name to a product? Why do speakers who are famous (or infamous) get astronomical speaking fees when they really aren't very good speakers? Why do well-known authors get huge advances on their planned books before they've even put pen to paper? (Note: no advance for this book.) Why is it that so much wealth and reward is concentrated in a disproportionately small group of people?

Clear explains the reason in his article by going back to nature. He uses the example of two plants growing side by side in the Amazon forest. They compete for sunlight, water, and safety from parasites and disease. If one gains an advantage over the other, it starts to overshadow its neighbor, and pretty soon the neighbor isn't getting the sunshine or water that is now being consumed by the faster-growing plant. As the plant grows stronger, it dominates. Pretty soon, the smaller plant is crowded out, withers, and dies. Now, there is even more space for the dominant species to spread its seeds and multiply.

Like plants, people compete. And like the plants, the rewards go to the winner; sometimes exponentially. Clear says in his article that *"…situations in which small differences in performance lead to outsized rewards are known as Winner-Take-All Effects."*

He's right.

Nations compete. Organizations compete. And, people compete. Those that rise to the top often dominate for quite some time. Look at Apple, Google, the New England Patriots, or the Golden State Warriors. Alabama and Clemson football. Look at the Roman Empire, the British Empire, or the United States since World War II.

Look at how Olympic athletes are able to market their success into follow-on careers. Some, like swimmers, sprinters, or downhill skiers, might have bested the Silver Medalist by just tenths of a second, yet their reward is outsized.

> *The classic type A person who is both ambitious and talented may rise above the rest because they have exponentially greater determination… a kind of inner "grit."*

The classic type A person who is both ambitious and talented may rise above the rest because they have exponentially greater determination… a kind of inner "grit." Extra effort can, and does, pay off, and often separates the good from the great, and the great from the truly great.

The point of the last chapter is that—at some point—we all reach a culmination place. Initial disappointment in stopping there shouldn't be overshadowed by a negative reflection on the tremendous journey experienced getting there. Reach for the stars, but be mindful of the fact that not everyone can be #1.

Finally, as you'll find out in Chapter 19, arrival at a particular rung on the ladder could come with great sacrifices that you might regret once you arrive.

Be careful what you wish for.

12

Change Happens!

"If you want to make God laugh,
tell him about your plans..."

Woody Allen

We have been living in a fast-moving world for at least a century. Hundreds of years ago, people lived their lives, and little changed from day to day. Today, one of the few predicable things is that change is constant and we must be prepared to not just accept it... but adapt and run with it.

Change can happen on the flip of a coin and you have to be ready to reconfigure plans. There's an old saying in the military that *"no plan survives first contact with the enemy."* Not recognizing the need to *plan for change* is a recipe for potential disaster. That's why the military has "branch and sequel" plans and "contingency" plans to supplement the base plan, and this is equally appropriate in the corporate world.

Here's a couple of instances when I had to go through significant change.

When I was in command of the 2nd Battalion, 10th Cavalry at Fort Knox, Kentucky, we participated in the same annual REFORGER exercise (discussed in Chapter 4) that I had participated in as a captain and major during two previous tours in Germany. This time, however, we deployed from the United States to Germany with all our staff, plus key command and control vehicles and other support equipment.

Since the early days of the Cold War, REFORGER had been a comprehensive all-in exercise with tanks and heavy weapons. This time, however, we went without the tanks and heavy vehicles. One reason for this was that a huge change had occurred in the world. The Berlin Wall fell in 1989 and people started thinking about a "peace dividend." Why would we need such a large European-based military if the Soviet Union had just collapsed? Expensive exercises that included shipping all of a unit's equipment over from the United States wasn't viewed as being as necessary or cost effective as it had been in past years.

At the end of the exercise, we found ourselves on the wash racks in Grafenwoehr, Germany, cleaning our vehicles and equipment. It was about 2 a.m. in January of 1990—with a freezing rain making our efforts even more miserable and numbing—when our brigade commander, Col. Don Smith, called all seven of his battalion commanders together to tell us that the Army would be downsizing, and one of the victims of this "reset" would be the 194th Separate Armor Brigade.

We were shocked.

He explained that our seven battalions—consisting of over 5,000 soldiers—would transition into a single combined arms task force of approximately 1,000 men. He then said: *"Craig Whelden will be the commander of this newly-formed task force."*

I went through very mixed emotions that night. I had just been knocked off one mountain, but immediately told I was about to climb another. I was tasked with converting a 450-man tank battalion to a 1,000-man combined arms task force of armor, infantry, and artillery. We were told to choose the best equipment to keep and select the highest quality soldiers with the most longevity from the other six battalions, to hold onto. My organization would go into a "Readiness Condition

5" status until the task force was formed, meaning that the Army would not levy requirements on us during this period of transition, which should last approximately a year.

On my return to Fort Knox, I set upon the

On my return to Fort Knox, I set upon the task of rearranging the deck chairs on the 194ᵗʰ Titanic.

task of rearranging the deck chairs on the 194ᵗʰ Titanic. As you can imagine, morale in the other battalions was not high. They were folding their flags and disbanding. My challenge was that, in forming a new team, I had to ensure it would become a cohesive group with a single purpose, not a collection of soldiers who wanted to live in the past and be somewhere else. I also had to spend the coming months inventorying equipment, determining what was best to keep, which soldiers to transfer in and out, and how to train a unit that would be unique in the Army. There was no other unit quite like what became "Task Force 1-10 Cavalry."

We were in the midst of this reorganization when, on August 2, 1990, Saddam Hussein invaded Kuwait.

The entire United States military now had to change its focus from decades of staring down the Soviet Union across the Iron Curtain to deploying to the Middle East to get ready to fight a desert war. Within days, the 82ⁿᵈ Airborne—one of the crack units of the Army—sent airborne troopers over to Saudi Arabia to block any penetration of Iraqi tanks, should they push south from Kuwait in order to take control of the Saudi ports so critical to our entry into the area. We may never know whether Saddam Hussein would have done this—absent these brave airborne soldiers—but some of us were thinking they would be little more than speed bumps on Saddam's road south, since they were so lightly armed.

General Gordon Sullivan was the Vice Chief of Staff of the Army at that time, and he visited Fort Knox to assess the readiness of the Armor force. He too was an Armor officer, and well understood what was required. When it was my time to brief, I informed him that we were in a Readiness Condition 5 status of transition and reorganization, but we still had equipment on Fort Knox. I offered that my former tank battalion could either be re-assembled and deployed or we could accelerate the reorganization and be ready to deploy very soon, despite not having trained the new task force as a unit. General Sullivan decided that we should continue the reorganization, but in the short term, I was directed to send my tank commanders to Dhahran, Saudi Arabia to become trainers for the U.S. tankers coming into the theater from other parts of the world.

The Army had brand new 120mm M1 Abrams tanks in storage in Europe, and these pristine-condition tanks would be brought to the Middle East to support the ground war. Much of the Armor force had not yet received this tank and was still using Abrams tanks with the 105mm gun. There was a need to train tankers on the differences between the two tanks, and my tank commanders became those trainers. The rest of my battalion would stay at Fort Knox to train returning Individual Ready Reserve soldiers who were being recalled to active duty for the war. These were soldiers who had recently left the service, but were still subject to recall.

Small Ways to Acknowledge the Past

While you may ask people to move on and forget how things were in the past, it can be useful to allow a small remnant of their former lives to remain.

I discovered several techniques for dealing with change during this time. First, while you may ask people to move on and forget how things were in the past, it can be useful to allow a small remnant of their former lives to remain. A good way to do this is through acknowledging and recognizing symbols of their past.

My challenge was making the men

from the seven disparate battalions feel like they were all part of the same newly-formed team. There were soldiers from two different tank battalions, one infantry battalion, one field artillery battalion, a maintenance and support battalion, a medical battalion, and an engineer battalion. Once they had been selected, it became clear that many lamented the fact that they were no longer identified with and by their former unit. Some felt that in joining this "hybrid" organization, they would lose their branch identity. I had to find a way to fix that.

One solution was to let the men literally wear their past on their uniforms. While everyone had to wear the crest of the 1st Battalion, 10th Cavalry on their headgear (hat), I allowed each of the infantry, artillery, and other branches to wear their former crest on their pocket lapels, signifying their association to their basic branch and their disbanded battalions. The Army is usually very particular about uniform standards and this was at odds with those standards. But I asked for and received permission to do this from my leadership.

If you are faced with a reorganization or significant transition that you have to lead people through, I suggest you find some type of symbol that people have strong feelings about and allow it to remain. It might be a flag, a former company logo, or an old mission statement. Whatever it is, let it help smooth the transition to whatever the change is leading you towards. View it as a bridge from the past to the future.

Another thing I did to help ease the transition was to create a formal ritual to help people embrace their new organization: a way to bond the team; to bring them together to recognize the worth and contribution of every individual towards the whole. I used such a ritual whenever we had a major training event for the new task force. We created a recognition ceremony conducted at sunset in torchlight formations, something I had seen films of the German Army doing in World War II. During these events, I recognized soldiers and small units from every prior battalion. I focused on *everyone*, going well beyond the traditional tankers, infantryman, and artillerymen to also recognize cooks, mechanics, and fuel and ammunition handlers who all played a role in any collective success.

It was a challenge to bring these disparate groups together, but when I turned over the unit colors to my replacement in July 1991, I felt like we had finally come together as a team, and every soldier was proud to be a member of Task Force 1-10 Cavalry.

Like me, they accepted that *change happens*, and they did just fine moving forward.

13

The Whole = the Sum of Its Parts

*"For the strength of the pack is the wolf, and
the strength of the wolf is the pack."*
Rudyard Kipling

It was during this time at Fort Knox, when we were fighting Desert Shield/Desert Storm, that I faced a leadership challenge anyone could face—how to manage the conflation of strong ambition with equally strong disappointment among the leaders in my task force. The military is full of brave young Americans eager to show they can take on any task, even when it risks their life.

The corporate world, too, is filled with ambitious, hard-charging people who want to demonstrate their business prowess, developing new products or opening new markets at great risk to the bottom line. In either case, a leader has to know how to work with these personalities; sometimes encouraging them, sometimes restraining them, but always supporting them.

I faced this challenge when I was in command of the task force described in the last chapter. It was an organization of nearly 1,000 men. Most of my 40+ officers—and many of the men under them—lamented the fact that they were not deploying for what they believed would be the greatest tank battle since World War II.

It was the "Super Bowl" and they were sitting on the bench.

In their view, other tank battalions in the Army would deploy to the Middle East and would return as heroes, able to wear the revered "combat patch" on their right sleeve, a sign of virility among soldiers, at a time when there hadn't been a big fight for many years. A combat patch made a statement all its own about *"I've been there... done that"* irrespective of how well it may have been done. No one in our battalion, that I remember, had a combat patch except Command Sergeant Major Jerry Utterback, who earned his in Vietnam.

Once my officers knew that they would not deploy to the Middle East, I realized that I had to assure them that they still served a valuable purpose in our Army and in support of the overall war effort. I explained that their job would be equally important—perhaps even more so—than some of those who crossed the Iraqi or Kuwaiti border. While I think there may have been some truth to this, I'm not sure my officers believed me at the time. Even I doubted what I was saying because I, too, was disappointed that we were staying back.

But I believe my words had a long-term effect on them, especially when I told them that if anyone in the battalion was to be professionally short-changed as a result of not deploying to Desert Shield/Desert Storm, it would be me. After all, I was already a lieutenant colonel and my professional path forward led through an ever-narrowing path of selection boards. The higher you rise in the ranks, the tougher it becomes to reach the next "rung on the ladder," as I wrote about earlier. My rungs were becoming further and further apart, and my professional future in the Army was even more uncertain now that I would be competing with "combat-experienced" battalion commanders for the next promotion or selection for command.

I assured my lieutenants and captains that their careers were not being jeopardized. Their careers wouldn't start becoming really "competitive" until they competed for resident attendance at Command and General Staff College. For most of them, this was still 5-10 years away. By that time, the war experience gained by others would be a faint memory to the board members selecting them. What really counted is how well they did *whatever* they were asked to do and *wherever* and *whenever* they were asked to do it.

Again, I'm not sure even I believed what I was saying, but I do believe my message resonated. And it turns out that I was spot on. The ground war lasted just 4 days, and while the deployment of other units to Saudi Arabia spanned many months, much of that time was spent getting ready—a fairly routine (and sometimes boring) task.

As I told my men, the fact that one is in a combat zone does not *per se* mean that they had a leg up on those who were not there. Everyone still had the same potential to be promoted. Selection boards understood this, at the time. Two lieutenants in the audience that day—John Epperly and John Andonie—now serve as Army General Officers.

Toxic Competition

In the same unit, I had a more localized experience that demonstrated how the "whole equals the sum of its parts" but, when separated and competing against each other, they can weaken the whole.

We were getting ready for a major gunnery training event, and I noticed what might be viewed as unhealthy competition among two of the tank company commanders. Each was determined to be the best company coming out of the gunnery event.

While I value healthy competition, I value teamwork even more.

From their perspective, they didn't see the value—as I did—of sharing good ideas or helping each other if it might give the other a leg up. I pulled them aside one day to reinforce the point that while I value healthy competition, I value teamwork even more. Ultimately, I would grade them on not just quantifiable gunnery scores, but also on how they worked together; how they shared good ideas; how they made each of the individual parts contribute to the whole: our entire battalion. It is the same principle I experienced in Ranger School years before, where "teamwork" became one of the most valued aspects of a student's evaluation.

One of Benjamin Franklin's oft-repeated quotes is: *"We must, indeed, all hang together or, most assuredly, we shall all hang separately."* Most of us don't experience the level of importance (national survival) that Franklin was referring to when he said this, but truly great leaders understand where the crossover point is between personal, and sometimes competing, ambitions of individuals versus the contributions of each as a member of a team to the collective good of the whole. There is room for both. Great leaders know where these sometimes-competing interests intersect.

Finally, I'm reminded of a TED Talk by Margaret Heffernan titled *"Why It's Time to Forget the Pecking Order at Work."* Her talk can easily be found on the internet and is an instructive lesson on the value of what bonds the whole together. She uses the metaphor of a brick wall, and when she says *"It's the mortar, not the bricks,"* she's referring to what holds us together that gives us strength, as opposed to the individual bricks.

I often refer to this TED presentation in my talks while displaying a photo of the Great Wall of China. Without the mortar—that which binds it together—it would be just a huge pile of bricks.

14

"Memento Mori"

"The supreme quality for leadership
is unquestionably integrity."
Dwight D. Eisenhower

I was about 18 months into command of the base in Wurzburg when I got a call from the 3rd Infantry Division Commander, Major General Montgomery (Monty) Meigs—my former boss in Schwabach years before—asking me to come up to the Division headquarters. He told me that the Chief of Staff of the Army had approved my leaving my command six months early to become his Chief of Staff, replacing a colonel who was being relieved for indiscretions with a subordinate civilian female employee. In the next few hours, I turned over my duties to my executive officer and moved up to the Division headquarters. The colonel I replaced had been my next-door neighbor, but he was gone in ten days, forced into retirement.

This kind of episode occurs too often. It's a failure of character and a stain on any profession. It reminds me of a story about how excessive hubris infects some people when they gain power.

A Roman general enters Rome after a large victory. Standing behind him on his chariot is his slave, tasked to remind the general that though he was at his peak today, tomorrow he could fall. The servant conveyed this by telling the general, *"Memento mori"*— literally, *"Remember, you are mortal."*

Ethical behavior should be non-negotiable. It pains me to see senior military officers and business executives in the news for violating this basic foundational principal of leadership. Power corrupts those of lesser character, and it can be a slippery slope if you find yourself getting away with behavior you should know is unacceptable. It feeds on itself and can be like a metastasizing cancer on the soul. I often wonder why and how this happens. It's particularly embarrassing to witness senior military leaders fail in this critical area of leadership in a profession that, year after year, is regarded as one of the most trusted institutions in America.

It is all the more important to remember *"memento mori"* as you rise in your organization and become a senior leader. Realize that as you climb the corporate ladder, you start to live in a glass house. Everyone is watching, and people will judge not only your words, but also your deeds. The world should never revolve around you. You are a servant leader. Practice humility, always adhere to high standards of integrity, and set the example in all you do. Keep in mind this statement from Albert Einstein: *"Whoever is careless with the truth in small matters cannot be trusted in important matters."*

World-renowned leadership author and speaker John C. Maxwell said: *"Your talk talks ... and your walk talks ... but your walk talks louder than your talk talks."* A tongue-twister for sure, but once dissected, it's clear what it means.

When I was promoted to brigadier general, I remember asking my boss, Major General John Van Alstyne, what was different about being a general. I felt exactly the way I did the day before, when I was a colonel. He said: *"Your jokes don't get any funnier... you don't get any better looking... and if it tastes good, spit it out."* Although humorous at first, there's deep meaning in that very sage advice. His point was clearly to not let elevation into the senior ranks go to my head. Temptations coming my way must be rejected. Two key and critical leadership traits were profiled to me that day: *humility* and *integrity*. These are just part of the elements of character—the building block of all great leaders—discussed in Chapter One.

For the past 20+ years, this has been the foundation of what I pass on to others who arrive at that same professional crossroads. Every year, I send a letter to newly selected generals – first in the Army, then in the Marine Corps—passing on this sage advice from John Van Alstyne.

What really counts is not the cheering crowd, but rather having a firm understanding of what the citizens actually say and think about you after your chariot passes.

Ethical Boundaries

What really counts is not the cheering crowd, but rather having a firm understanding of what the citizens actually say and think about you after your chariot passes.

When I was a General Officer, one of the things I did regularly was gather together my immediate and closest staff members (aide, secretary, driver, etc.) and tell them that I would never cross an ethical boundary intentionally. Because of my position, though, I would often be put in circumstances that could pull me in that direction—unknowingly—and the last thing I wanted to do was to find myself on the other side wondering how I got there. I picked up this "rock" from Major General Meigs when I was his chief of staff.

Because these were the members of my team that spent most of their time with me, I charged each of them to *"keep their antennae up"* for these kinds of situations and say something if they saw us drifting in that direction. I then turned to my lawyer—who was in attendance—to let him tell everyone present exactly where those boundaries were. I've seen a number of General Officers use a technique similar to this. Not only does it keep you "inside the boundaries," but it sets the bar for your entire organization regarding where you stand on ethical behavior.

And… it often sets the same bar for them.

15

Managing Risk

"Being a Navy SEAL and sniper taught me all about risk management. Take away all the risk variables under your control and reduce it to an acceptable level. The same fundamentals apply in business."

Brandon Webb

One of the key elements of leadership is helping your company, your team, or your family navigate risks. It's a volatile and chaotic world, and leaders must know how to face risks and survive. You may need to make decisions for which there are known financial risks, new product or service risks, competitive risks, or even the risk of physical harm to your people or your family. We all also face risks that cannot be calculated in advance and for which we are thus unable to prepare.

I have encountered a few risks in my life and have learned something from each of them that I will explore in this chapter. I believe my experiences with getting through risky situations have contributed to making me a more effective leader.

Risk Lesson #1 - Life Experiences Help Shape Your Appreciation of Risk

Humans are not born with natural instincts or skills about how to recognize or handle risks. As children, our brains are naturally inclined to believe that the world is safe and that we can conquer most things we encounter. Children often feel they can get away with anything, until something happens that teaches them otherwise, or parents intervene. Ironically, while humans are the most advanced species in the animal kingdom, we seem to be the slowest to appreciate the dangers around us. That's why we must be nurtured for such a long time before setting off on our own.

I was just six years old when I had my first near-death experience. My father was in the Air Force and stationed in England, and my family was on a vacation in Switzerland. We were high in the Jungfrau mountain range when I strayed off the beaten path and fell into a 30-foot snow crevice. Bravely, my dad jumped in after me, but only succeeded in trapping us both 30 feet down. Hours later, we were fortunately pulled out by Swiss mountain rescue teams—in good shape, but extremely cold. We later learned that had I continued falling about two more feet beyond where I stopped, I would have dropped another 200-300 feet, certainly to my death. On that day, I did not understand the life-threatening situation in which I put myself and my father. I remember telling my mom afterwards that I lost a red mitten in the crevice, as if suggesting she should go retrieve it.

I tested fate a few more times before turning 20 years old. One of the most serious was just after my freshman year in college. I spent time in southern England working at Camp Mohawk during my high school years and into college. This was a youth camp on the Salisbury Plain near Stonehenge, England and was a wonderful place where children of the U.S. military from throughout Europe could spend a few weeks each summer. I had been a camper there myself when I was seven or eight years old.

*In addition to other duties, I was an American
Indian dancer at Camp Mohawk - 1968*

After my senior year in high school, the camp's director asked me to run the *Whitewater Canoe Teenage Adventure Trip* when I returned the following summer, following my freshman year at Purdue. This trip would take about 30 teenagers, ages 14-16, downstream on the Wye River in Wales, spanning a 10-day period. At the time, I was just 17 and had not yet received my driver's license. Not realizing the enormity of the responsibilities I would inherit… and apparently the camp director not recognizing the liabilities he might incur... I readily agreed, as it seemed like another great adventure.

Another mountain to climb.

I spent the summer of 1969 as an apprentice (called "right-seating") with the outgoing trip leader to learn the river for the following summer, when I would be in charge. What I didn't know during these trial runs was that the river was unusually low that summer. This training trip was uneventful and great fun.

Right-seating on the Wye River with Bill Anderson - 1969

The following spring, however—a few months before I started leading the trips myself—Wales had record rainfall. When I arrived back from my freshman year in college in the summer of 1970, the water on the Wye River was exceptionally high. Safety protocols for our trip required that we pull up just short of each set of rapids, beach the canoes, walk to the edge of the river overlooking the rapids, and talk through our strategy to get through them.

Once the group understood how to get through, a safety officer with a rope was placed downstream, and the group would observe me going through, first. Once through, I would disembark, then oversee and supervise each of the remaining 2-person canoes through the rapids, one at a time.

At 18 years old and responsible for the lives of 30 teenagers, I thought I knew what I was doing. However, the river looked very different than the year before. Most of the landmarks I had carefully marked on the map and memorized were now underwater and couldn't be seen. When we approached the first set of rapids, I didn't see expected landmarks. Some were submerged. We were quickly pulled into the main current. There was no turning back or pulling over to the side, so I looked over my shoulder and yelled for the seven canoes behind to *"Follow me!"* We all had life vests, but rapids are dangerous, nonetheless.

Of the eight canoes, six made it through. Two did not. The four teenagers in those two canoes were upended and thrown into the cold water, racing downriver. One of the canoes hit a boulder, spun around, and got locked onto a second boulder. It was caught in a chute that had a depth of about five feet. Fortunately, the four canoers managed to find their way to calmer water and extract themselves to the bank. All were safe, but I felt terrible that we had an expensive aluminum canoe locked between two large boulders, facing upriver, with the rushing water holding it fast.

This is when I made the fateful decision to "recover the canoe," as I couldn't imagine returning to Camp Mohawk one canoe short. I didn't pause to assess my chances, nor did I recall my falling through the crack in the mountains in Switzerland a dozen years before. Instead, I selected the largest and strongest teenager to help me retrieve the canoe. We went upriver to a point where we could float downstream, hopefully landing on the stuck canoe. We removed our life vests so their bulk wouldn't interfere with our manual work to free the canoe.

You're now probably wondering, *"What was he thinking?"*

In retrospect, I wasn't.

Once at the canoe, we braced ourselves against the boulders and rocked the canoe back and forth until one end finally gave and the strong current began carrying it downriver. I yelled at the teenager to *"Grab the canoe!"* as it was buoyant and would keep him above water. He did so.

I then lunged for the canoe myself... but missed and found myself at the mercy of the currents, and—yes—without a life jacket. The next few minutes are a fog. I recall only being dragged by the gushing water over boulders, completely losing my orientation, and not finding air. I was running out of breath, and for an instant, I thought this was the end. I eventually found the surface, gasping to fill my lungs, and was able to find my way to calmer waters. I was exhausted and had no feeling in my legs.

Despite little strength and without the use of my legs, I managed to drag myself to the side of the river and lay there for what seemed an eternity until the numbness subsided. The kids found me and helped me recover. But we now had only seven of the eight canoes. The eighth was found two days later 10 miles downriver, trapped in a downed tree. Meanwhile, the aluminum body of the canoe we had freed was torn and banged up beyond use. I took it back to Camp Mohawk at the end of this trip, but had a difficult and embarrassing time explaining to the camp director what happened.

With this "out of the chute" experience behind me, the following two canoe trips I led that summer were uneventful, but I learned a powerful lesson about risk ... one that has stayed with me since. I often talk about it when giving talks to groups about risk analysis and management. The takeaway for leaders is that you cannot assume that your people—especially young people—truly understand and appreciate the nature of risk. People far too often fail to recognize an obvious risk when it is sometimes staring them in the face. Leaders must be constantly vigilant and open the eyes of their team to the many known risks surrounding them, ensuring they understand them. Then, they must develop a plan to mitigate those risks.

Risk Lesson #2 - Use the Proper Equipment and Follow Safety Protocols

Every time you get into a car, (I hope) you put on your seatbelt. That's because you know it makes sense to use the equipment designed to reduce your risk of dying in an accident. Unfortunately, I've witnessed too many tragic accidents in the military when soldiers did not use equipment properly or neglected to follow established safety protocols and procedures.

I recall a very tragic incident when I was a tank platoon leader at Fort Hood, Texas in the mid-70s. Field operations involving tanks are dangerous. The tank itself was a 52-ton behemoth and fraught with risk, whether conducting live fire exercises or just moving it across a motor pool. In one field exercise, my unit was on some high ground, in a defensive position, waiting to be assaulted by the opposition in a force-on-force exercise.

In the early morning hours of the fourth day, a tank from another platoon was moving along the ridge, and got too close to the edge. The right track found its way over the precipice, resulting in the tank tipping over and rolling to the bottom, killing a lieutenant inside.

Tanks in those days had a seat for the commander that was normally kept in a stored position above the radio. It was affectionately called the "autobahn seat" because it was only supposed to be used when conducting long marches on flat roads or highways, where there is less risk. (Autobahns are the major highways of Germany.)

On a training exercise at Fort Hood - 1974

But in this incident, the lieutenant had the autobahn seat locked in place, with the upper half of his body protruding from the tank commander's cupola. He didn't have time to get the seat properly stored as his tank went over the edge. The rest of his crew, though banged up, survived. When I later saw this tank in our motor pool, its top was covered by the remains of this unfortunate young officer.

During my three years at Fort Hood, there were other incidents of soldiers sleeping on the ground who were run over by tanks in the middle of the night because their area was not adequately marked or guarded.

In another tragic incident, a tank in a motor pool had just finished being cleaned with high-pressure hoses and was being moved over to the maintenance bay for some routine maintenance. One of the crewmembers was on the ground guiding his tank, motioning to the driver which way to turn and when to stop. Violating procedures, he placed himself between the tank and a building, and when he motioned for the tank to stop, the driver pressed the brake; but, with wet boots from the tank washing, his foot slipped off the brake and the tank continued to roll forward, pinning the ground guide against the building and killing him.

In all these cases, appropriate risk management was not done. In the first case, the lieutenant was not using the equipment properly, and in the other cases, soldiers were not following established safety protocols. Sadly, all these incidents resulted in deaths that did not have to happen. All the participants were young; still teenagers or in their early 20s. They were also very inexperienced, not having been in the Army more than a couple of years.

Tragically, leaders are too often unaware that their team members are not using the tools correctly or following appropriate safety protocols. Though we can't be everywhere for every risky situation, we should realize when risks are rising and then prepare our people—particularly the young and inexperienced ones—by insisting they pay attention to the right way to use their equipment and that they follow safety rules. Sometimes, extra layers of supervision are appropriate.

Lesson #3 - Risks Show Up from Nowhere... Often When Least Expected

While still a ROTC cadet at Purdue, I attended the three-week Airborne School at Fort Benning, Georgia to learn how to parachute from military aircraft. Some might ask why a future Armor officer would need to jump out of airplanes, but the 82d Airborne Division had, in that day, a tank battalion that dropped tanks from aircraft. In addition, we never knew when a soldier—of any type—might be assigned to the staff of an airborne unit.

For me, at 20 years old, it was just another adventure... another mountain to climb.

Those who have never done a military jump need to appreciate that the goal is to get jumpers on the ground as fast as possible. As such, the height from which the jump is made is much lower (1,200 feet in training and 800 feet in combat) than civilian jumps, and the military parachute is designed to move through the air at maximum speed, but within risk tolerance to the jumper. You hit the ground relatively hard, so perfecting the "PLF" (Parachute Landing Fall) is essential.

On one of my jumps, I witnessed a phenomenon that stays with me to this day. With several hundred jumpers in the air at any given time, the sky becomes very crowded. Students are told to give wide berth to other jumpers. If you drift over the top of another jumper, you can find yourself in a vacuum with no air to sustain your chute. On my third jump, I saw this occur. Another jumper drifted over the top of another chute and the air keeping his chute open disappeared. His chute collapsed and he flew past the jumper below him. Once past, the air caught his chute and it re-opened, but now the other jumper was above him, and *his* chute lost its air.

I don't recall how many times I saw this "leapfrog" occur, but the two jumpers could not get away from each other, and one of them reached the ground before his chute fully re-deployed. He broke both legs and didn't graduate. I don't know if he ever returned to try again.

Another incident at jump school taught me something about risk, as well. As mentioned earlier, my dad flew C47s in the early 50s in support of the Airborne School. The outside skin of a C47 is full of rivets, including surrounding the door that jumpers exit. Students are told to put their hands on the outside of the aircraft and pull themselves out to help propel the body beyond the side of the aircraft and into the wind stream.

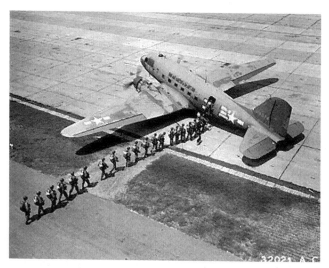

Loading airborne students in the early 50s

My dad was piloting an aircraft when a jumper caught his wedding ring on a rivet while exiting the door. He left his ring finger on the aircraft as his body dropped to earth. Because of this, my dad never wore a wedding ring, much to the chagrin of my mother. He told me this story before I attended Jump School, and while I didn't have any rings then, I found myself checking the hands of my airborne classmates to ensure they didn't, either.

My nephew, Jason Dixon, had a similar experience. In 2008, he was attending the Warrant Officer Basic Course at Quantico Marine Corps Base, Virginia. A physically demanding course, it includes a long obstacle course with an eight-foot wall that students had to go over. On one of these training events, he jumped up to grab the top of the wall, pulled himself up, and dropped to the far side. Regrettably, he was wearing his wedding ring and his finger stayed at the top of the wall. A nail was protruding just enough to catch his ring. Because Jason was in excellent physical condition, he was kept in the course even though he did no further obstacle course runs. He graduated two months later—minus one finger.

Today, as part of the safety orientation for incoming students, a photo of Jason's four-fingered left hand is shown to incoming students—with the official story of how it happened. There are a number of unofficial stories how he lost his finger, as well. For a while, his youngest son believed it was lost in a bear fight... which Jason obviously won.

My Conclusions about Risk

I long ago learned that it was my job to teach others—especially young people—about risk and ensure that they take the right precautions to minimize it.

All these experiences have made me far more aware of risks. I long ago learned that it was my job to teach others—especially young people—about risk and ensure that they take the right precautions to minimize it. Risk management is now second nature.

The military has a simple five step process that can be applied in combat and in training. It can also be applied in business or in your daily life. Anyone can use this simple tool regularly whenever facing risks. It has served me well and it can do the same for you.

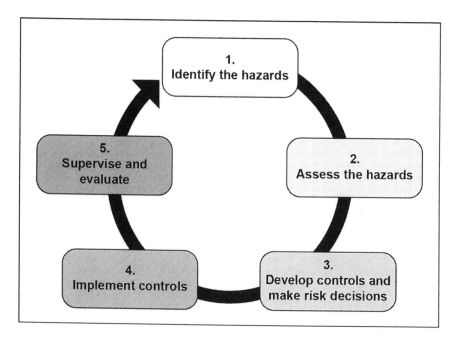

As the years have passed, I've also reflected on the psychic makeup of teenagers and young adults and the risks they are sometimes willing to take. This is especially important in the military, with such a large demographic between 18-22 years old, coupled with the inherent adventurism of young people who join the military. It is also true for many businesses that employ young Millennials fresh out of high school or college.

Research has shown that the human brain continues to develop well into early adulthood. The pre-frontal cortex, which starts development around puberty, isn't completely formed until about age 25. This portion of the brain controls impulse inhibition, goal planning, and organization. It also feeds a "reward system" that results in young adults under 25 often taking unnecessary risks because, in their mind, the rewards are worth the risk. This was the case for me when I was trying to free the canoe in the rapids of the Wye River.

Paradoxically, this lack of experience with risk is why young people make good soldiers or marines, but it's also why we lose too many of them to avoidable accidents. They are willing to put their lives at stake for their country, and take far bigger risks than older people would typically take.

This is precisely why it is a leader's responsibility to assess the level of risk using tools similar to the one described above, incorporate mitigations as needed, and then supervise the execution to ensure that risk and reward are in the appropriate balance.

Don't risk not doing so...

16

Stepping up in Times of Crisis

"When written in Chinese, the word 'crisis'
is composed of two characters...
One represents danger and the other
represents opportunity."
President John F. Kennedy

There are times when you, as a leader, must reach deep into your soul and take charge of what already is or will soon become a serious crisis for your organization. These episodes may be far and few between, but you need to be prepared for them psychologically, intellectually, and operationally.

Some leaders never give a thought to what they would need to do or how they might need to react should a true crisis threaten their organization. But if you are not prepared to assess the situation, know your options, and make decisions, you might risk harm to your people, your assets, and even your survivability. People depend on you to lead them through a crisis, and sometimes it means dealing with situations you never imagined you would encounter and developing new skills that you didn't know you had. I experienced this once, and it is a story worth telling.

For many Americans, 9/11 was such a crisis. I happened to be in Washington D.C. that fateful day at an Army Installations Conference being held in a hotel just across the highway from the Pentagon. The circumstances of my being there were eerily coincidental, as I was stationed in Hawaii at the time, not in Washington D.C.

At that time, I was the Deputy Commander of U.S. Army Pacific, and part of my responsibilities included oversight of base operations in the Pacific. The conference was being held at the DoubleTree Hotel just across from Interstate 395, the main artery into Washington D.C. coming from the south. This highway is about the only thing that separated the hotel from the Pentagon.

The Assistant Chief of Staff for Installation Management (ACSIM) was the Army's senior staff officer charged with the resourcing and running of Army bases. At that time, the ACSIM was Major General Robert "Van" Van Antwerp, my former boss from my time running Army morale, welfare, and recreation programs. His offices were in the Pentagon, but on this day, there were dozens of his staff members over at the DoubleTree.

That morning, we were assembled in a basement conference room and had just started our meeting when someone came into the room to announce that a plane hit one of the World Trade Center towers. At the time, no one could fully ascertain the circumstances, so we didn't react. Like the rest of the country, everyone believed it was accidental.

But not long after, another person rushed in to announce that a second plane had hit the other tower. Now we knew that this was no accident. We asked the hotel to bring a television into our conference room so we could monitor the situation in New York, and someone established contact with the Army Operations Center in the Pentagon.

Then, at 9:37 a.m.—just 34 minutes after the 2nd World Trade Center tower was hit—American Airlines Flight 77 hit the Pentagon. As close as we were, we did not hear the impact because our meeting room was in the basement. Soon, someone ran into the room to tell us that *"There has been an explosion over at the Pentagon."*

We all ran outside to see a black plume of smoke rising from the Pentagon. At that time, we didn't know exactly where the plane had hit, but we later learned that ground zero was precisely where General Van Antwerp's new offices were located. Two secretaries manning the phones were killed, but dozens from that office survived because they were in the DoubleTree Hotel with us.

We were all angry and confused. How could anyone mount an attack of this scale with box cutters and airline tickets?

Protecting the homeland was underpinned at that time by a nuclear triad: ground, sea, and air-based missiles designed to deter an adversary from launching an attack against our homeland. We had spent billions over the past decades to assure such deterrence. I knew this deterrence well, since—just a few years before—I had worked in the National Military Command Center as one of the one-star duty officers responsible to the Secretary of Defense and the President of the United States for nuclear response. I wore a key around my neck that, when simultaneously turned with my Deputy's key, could start World War III and possibly assure the world's destruction. For years, we had been looking outward to detect any threats... not inward.

This was sure to be a different kind of war; one we were less prepared for.

My first instinct was to call my wife in Hawaii because she knew I was meeting with an office based in the Pentagon. It was approaching 10 a.m. on the East coast, so it was only 4 a.m. in Hawaii. I couldn't get through on my cell, so I ran up to my hotel room and called her on the landline. I woke her up, told her I was OK, and asked that she call both my headquarters and my parents in Indianapolis. Later, I found that I had notified Karen even before the Hawaii Governor found out, since our national civil defense notification system was untried and rusty.

I then rushed over to the Pentagon to see what I could do to help.

I saw a gaping hole, but the windows just either side of it were eerily intact. Oddly, windows further away from the impact zone were gone, and both fire and smoke were coming out of these more distant windows. I later learned this was because a section of the building recently renovated and strengthened to protect against terrorist attack was exactly where the airplane had hit. The windows further away had not yet been changed, so the concussion had blown them out, while the closer windows to the point of impact remained intact.

The Pentagon, after the attack on 9/11

Standing in front of the impact zone that first morning, it wasn't clear to me who was in charge. First responders from multiple agencies and jurisdictions had arrived at the scene. The immediate task was putting out the fire and rescuing survivors, so I approached the Arlington County Fire Chief and asked him what help he needed. He told me he could use some "blocking and bracing material" to shore up the sides of the building so that once the fire was under control, they could enter and look for survivors and victims.

I contacted the nearby 3rd Infantry Regiment, "The Old Guard" (best known for their highly choreographed rifle drill and ceremonies, guarding the Tomb of the Unknown Soldier, and providing dignified services at military burials in Arlington National Cemetery), and asked them to provide needed assistance. Most people don't realize that this elite unit also has a wartime mission and is highly trained in combat operations. An engineer company is part of the 3rd Infantry Regiment and was ideally suited to provide the assistance requested by the fire chief.

About two hours after my phone call to my wife, I was standing next to an FBI agent when Army trucks started to roll across the field in front of the impact zone. When he saw this, and because I was a uniformed Army General Officer, he turned to me to ask who they were and *"...why are they driving across my crime scene?"* I explained that these were engineers bringing materials to be used by the fire chief to brace portions of the building to render it safer for rescue or recovery of victims inside. I could sense his focus was "investigative," while the fire chief's was "incident response"—two very different reactions to the same event — so I encouraged him to recognize that the fire chief's view was the higher priority.

I could sense his focus was "investigative," while the fire chief's was "incident response"–two very different reactions to the same event

Some time that morning, someone yelled on a bullhorn for everyone to move away from the Pentagon, as there were reports of another plane headed our way. We all moved back until the all-clear was given. We later learned that this alert was prompted by United Airlines (UA) Flight 93, which was ultimately taken down by passengers in Shanksville, Pennsylvania.

Later that day, I was standing next to another FBI Agent and asked him if he was aware of any centralized command center that had been established. He told me the Arlington County Sheriff's command van had been set up near the Navy Annex within a mile of where we were standing. He said he was about to go up there and asked if I'd like to accompany him.

I did, and when I got into his black SUV, I noticed multiple antennae on the top. When I asked what he did, he said he worked in "counter-terrorism." He also told me there was a fourth plane believed to be headed to Camp David, but that it had been "shot down." I later learned this was UA 93, that had prompted the bullhorn warning a while earlier.

This exchange reinforced for me that early reports in a crisis are often wrong, something I had learned in my military career over and over. Nevertheless, my first thought was to wonder, in the days that followed, whether there was developing a governmental cover-up about how UA 93 was taken down. Ultimately, I became convinced that it was Todd Beamer and other brave Americans who took the plane down and probably saved hundreds of people, as that plane was clearly headed for Washington D.C.

Interrogations with terrorists later captured, who had knowledge of the 9/11 planning, indicated that the two targets in Washington D.C. were the White House and the Capitol, not the Pentagon. American Airlines Flight 77, the one that hit the Pentagon, was probably targeting the White House, and United Airlines Flight 93 was headed to the Capitol when it crashed in Pennsylvania.

Here's why:

Flying into Reagan National Airport, the Capitol can clearly be seen from the air at a distance—at the opposite end of the mall from the Washington Monument. The White House is much smaller, harder to see, and is nestled in an area surrounded by buildings and trees. Radar tracking of Flight 77 showed that as it neared Washington D.C., it turned hard right and into almost a full (330 degree) circle as it approached, losing altitude along the way. The terrorists in the cockpit, with rudimentary knowledge of how to fly a large airplane at over 500 mph and unfamiliar with the landscape below, probably couldn't find the White House until it was too late to change the course of a much larger and faster plane than the piper cub they had trained on in Florida.

Once they realized they were not on a path to the White House, they tried to reposition the aircraft, but it was too late. Losing altitude, the Pentagon became the new target. I'm sure they didn't know that the Pentagon was in the midst of a very expensive, multi-year renovation, and one of the only sections that had been completed by 9/11 was the side they ultimately hit. This was a reinforced concrete structure with thickened mylar-covered windows that previously had been 1940s brick and mortar and simple glass panes. Had the airplane hit a side that was not recently reinforced, it likely would have penetrated deeper into the center of the building and killed many more people.

Many offices were vacant because staffs had been temporarily transferred to local Arlington and Alexandria spaces pending the renovation's completion. This is one of the reasons why the death toll was relatively low given the magnitude of the attack and the population density of the target area. There were just 189 deaths from this horrendous attack: 125 in the Pentagon and 64 in the aircraft. To provide context, the Pentagon had approximately 18,000 workers present that day, and before the renovation was started, the population numbered over 22,000.

If the Pentagon was actually the primary target, and the terrorists had done their homework, the bull's-eye would likely have been the River Entrance side where most of the senior leadership of our military had offices in the outer ring.

The Chief of Staff of the Army was not in Washington D.C. on 9/11. General Shinseki was in Singapore attending the Pacific Area Military Symposium. A plane nicknamed the *Grey Ghost* (and normally operated by the U.S. Marine Corps out of Hawaii) was dispatched to return him to Washington D.C.

The "Grey Ghost" - 2017

It arrived in D.C. on the 13th of September, and that evening I boarded the *Grey Ghost* to accompany it back to Hawaii. That was on a Thursday, and only military aircraft and a few charter planes were in the air, as the FAA's grounding of most commercial aircraft was not lifted until Friday, the 14th of September. (Ironically, ten years later, I was to find myself sitting in the same seat on the *Grey Ghost* during trips to Japan, Guam, and Australia, accompanying the commanding general of U.S. Marine Corps Forces Pacific as the senior civilian in the Marine Corps west of the Mississippi River.)

I landed back in Hawaii on Friday, the 14th of September, and found that Admiral Dennis Blair, Commander of U.S. Pacific Command, had given orders to the U.S. Army Pacific to lead and coordinate the effort to protect the state of Hawaii. My boss was Lieutenant General Ed Smith, and he passed to me the responsibility of overseeing this effort.

It was through these information and intelligence gaps that the terrorist-piloted airplanes flew.

Recall that in 2001, there was no Department of Homeland Security; in fact, there was not much at all connecting all the various agencies charged with protecting the homeland. It was through these information and intelligence gaps that the terrorist-piloted airplanes flew.

Given there was no coordinated and centralized guidance coming out of the federal government at that time, I sensed very strongly that we were largely on our own. As such, we created some innovative and creative new processes and procedures for the state's protection that became significant enough to receive national attention.

Just a few months after 9/11, General William Crouch, U.S. Army (Retired), and Admiral Harold Gehman, U.S. Navy (Retired), were in Hawaii to brief U.S. Pacific Fleet on their findings related to the attack on the USS Cole in Yemen in October of 2000. I had worked for General Crouch twice before, when he commanded the 2nd Armored Cavalry Regiment and I was in 1/1 Cavalry doing the Czech border mission in the mid-1980s, and again when he commanded U.S. Army Europe and I was one of his base commanders.

I invited General Crouch to the U.S. Army Pacific headquarters to learn what we were doing to protect Hawaii. After hearing our story, he suggested I share what we were doing with the rest of the country, because most state and local agencies were still struggling with how to prepare.

In March 2002, I wrote an article entitled *"Hawaii's Homeland Security,"* now easily found on the web. I was later invited to Washington D.C. to brief these innovative security initiatives to the new Office of Homeland Security, quickly formed by the Bush administration as a stopgap measure until a department could be fully established through Congress, 15 months after 9/11. Working with state, local, and federal agencies to protect the state of Hawaii from terrorist attack became a primary focus of mine for the next two years.

Deputy Commander, U.S. Army Pacific - 2003

A Post-script on my Role on Terrorism

I offer an additional quirky story about my role in the war against terror in the early years. The U.S. military went into Afghanistan very soon after 9/11. In the first few months, we were taking in Taliban and Al-Qaeda prisoners with few places to put them. Two candidate locations were chosen by the Department of Defense to house prisoners of war: Guantanamo Bay in Cuba and the island of Tinian in the Commonwealth of Northern Mariana Islands (CNMI), just north of Guam.

Tinian is one of three populated islands in the CNMI; it has about 2,000 inhabitants. In World War II, it was used as the base from which the U.S. launched B29s to bomb Japan. At one point, it was known as the busiest "airport" in the world. It is also the place from which the *Enola Gay* loaded the first atomic bomb and then flew to Hiroshima where it was dropped. The second atomic bomb was also loaded on Tinian and dropped on Nagasaki.

The Department of Defense leased two-thirds of the island in the 1980s for 100 years. The original idea was to build a B52 bomber base there to support the Cold War effort in the Pacific. That plan was scrapped, and little was done with the leased land. That meant there was plenty of space to put a prison and scarce opportunity for prisoners to escape.

It was a long swim to anywhere.

Admiral Blair gave my boss a warning order that if the POW camp was to come our way, the Army would build and run the prison. General Smith told me that if that happened, I would likely be its first camp commandant. I was about two weeks away from making my first trip to Tinian to do an initial site survey when Guantanamo Bay was chosen as the location for the prison. I cancelled my plans and thought, *"I guess I'll never see Tinian."*

As you read in Chapter 9, I was wrong. I've been to Tinian over a dozen times in recent years.

17

Celebrating Milestones and Victories

"Celebrate your successes. Find some humor in your failures."

Sam Walton

With your personal vision and your team's hard work, your leadership hopefully results in achieving many new milestones and victories for the organization. These are often moments to be celebrated. People need such celebration milestones, as it often "completes a circle."

I am referring to the circle of receiving an assignment or challenge, making plans, doing the work, putting out the effort, and finally achieving the desired result. When this complete circle occurs, it is vital and fitting to pause and recognize all that you have accomplished. You are back to the top of the circle, ready to receive a new assignment.

As I recounted earlier in the book about my use of ritual and ceremony during transition times to connect my soldiers' past and present, I also used ritual and ceremony to celebrate victories.

Let me relate one of those times when I was the Deputy Commanding General of the U.S. Army Pacific. In that position, one of the collateral duties I had was overseeing the chemical demilitarization operation on Johnston Island, 800 miles southwest of Hawaii. At the end of the Cold War, the United States had thousands of chemical weapons—mines, artillery shells, etc.—stockpiled at remote places across the United States. For most of the 1990s, we had been destroying these mines and shells at various locations across the United States. Johnston Island was one of those sites.

The island was originally an atoll one-tenth its current size, but engineers dredged the surrounding shallow sea bed decades before and enlarged the island enough to put an airfield there. It was a logical choice to use this island as a location to destroy chemical weapons, since there was no population there.

Johnson Island, about 800 miles SW of Hawaii

I periodically visited the island to inspect the operation and to recognize the dedicated employees charged with this hazardous duty. The facility was a self-contained structure with conveyor belts, drills, and furnaces, all controlled remotely behind sealed walls and windows. A mine or shell would be placed at the entrance of the facility and carried through on a conveyor belt. Automated machinery would then drill a hole in the shell and blast the chemical with high-temperature flames, burning it. The ensuing smoke and residue would then be filtered before escaping the building, where its toxicity was measured closely.

The facility had been in operation for nine years, and it was during my time that the last of the mines and shells were disposed of. We decided to celebrate this milestone, thereby recognizing the hard work and dedication that had been put out by the staff over the previous decade. A few dedicated souls had been there the entire duration of the mission.

I flew out to Johnston Island to be present for this historic moment, as did the official in Washington D.C. charged with all such chemical demilitarization operations across the country. The last chemical mine went through the furnace late one night in December 2000. There was no champagne to uncork, but speeches were made to recognize the service and sacrifice of employees present and past who had worked at Johnston Island for the past decade. We created a small commemorative gift that was given to each member present. Mine sits behind my desk today.

People will appreciate you more as a leader if you regularly celebrate their victories.

18

The Light at the End of the Tunnel

"Trust your landmark and run through the smoke. It's going to open up eventually."

Ezekiel Elliot

Often, people find themselves lost or going in the wrong direction in their lives. They become depressed, angry, and unable to figure out how to fix their immediate circumstances. It's like entering into a dark tunnel without knowing how long it is, or even doubting whether there's an exit.

Leaders can play a strong role in helping people regain their footing and rediscover their way. Everyone enters one or more of these tunnels sooner or later. I've been in them many times, myself. Sometimes the tunnels are long, but more often than not, you can find an exit and things turn out just fine.

Sometimes... life even improves.

Patience, fortitude, and perseverance often win out. Having someone help you navigate through the tunnel also helps.

Young people in particular—many of whom have not faced a major crisis in their life—often struggle to see their way through these tunnels. Some decide to take the easy way out by taking their own life. Suicides are particularly tragic, as there is often light at the end of the tunnel, but the affected individual just can't see it. I have seen this too often in the military—mostly with young people who simply do not have the long-term perspective that life can improve for them. My own sister took her life on Christmas Eve, 1999, a personal loss I'll address more in the next chapter.

> *Great leaders almost instinctively demonstrate how much they care about their people. It is part of who they are.*

Great leaders almost instinctively demonstrate how much they care about their people. It is part of who they are. Truly great leaders seem to know exactly when to apply this skill at the right moment and in the right way.

Let me relate a story of how I learned about the critical role that leaders play when it comes to guiding others through the dark tunnels of life.

Soon after I started my military career, I married my college sweetheart. I met her in the spring of 1972, when I was a junior at Purdue. After graduation in 1973, I went to Fort Hood, and she joined me in the spring of 1974, where she got her first exposure to military life.

Two years later, my marriage ended. I was 24 years old and was crushed. It was the first deep personal failure I had ever experienced, and I went into a very dark tunnel.

At the time, I was the maintenance officer for a tank battalion. One of my coping mechanisms was to invest any discretionary time and energy I had into my work. I spent many nights in the motor pool, sometimes doing anything to keep my mind focused.

One Friday night at about 7 p.m., when I was doing paperwork, completely alone except for the motor pool guards, I got a surprise visit. The Brigade Commander, Col. Jack Woodmansee, walked in. He was a former White House Fellow and a brilliant leader. He commanded roughly 4,000 soldiers, of which I was just one. From the point of view of a first lieutenant, the Brigade Commander was like *God*. Because he was many levels above me, we had never met.

Col. Woodmansee said he'd like me to join him in a walk through the motor pool. I was sure this was the perfect storm of bad luck: my marriage was falling apart, I was coping by investing my time in my work after hours, and now the Brigade Commander was going to inspect the motor pool... on a Friday night, no less. For the next 20-30 minutes, he and I walked up and down the tank lines.

Oddly, he never said a word about the status of maintenance, the appearance of the tanks, or anything remotely related to my job. Rather, he talked about challenges *he* had faced in life and how he got through them. He never mentioned my own situation, but when we finally got back to the front gate, he put his hand on my shoulder and said: *"There's light at the end of this tunnel; you just can't see it yet."*

I later learned that my battalion commander had told Col. Woodmansee about a young lieutenant who was facing difficult personal challenges and could use some encouragement. That is what brought the colonel to the motor pool that Friday evening.

Since that day, my memory has faded about a number of things and experiences, but that small but thoughtful gesture by a senior leader to a young officer buried deep in his own personal problems is seared into my memory like it was yesterday. I can't tell you how much his short visit lifted my spirits. Somebody cared when I felt like nobody did.

One often feels alone when things are going wrong. I put that rock in my backpack, and over the past 40 years, I've applied this same tactic a number of times, with similar success, on young people I have seen struggling.

Exiting the Tunnel

Making it through the tunnel sometimes seems impossible when you are in it, but I've learned that most tunnels have an exit. You generally find a solution to problems, and you should never give up hope, or stop trying to find the exit.

I left Fort Hood about 4 months after the "buck-up" talk from the colonel to attend the Armor Officer Advanced Course at Fort Knox, Kentucky. In May of 1977, 10 months after my divorce, I met Karen Lusk, who became my wife of over 41+ years. Ours was a whirlwind courtship that lasted just two months, and has persevered all these years. We have a wonderful son and daughter, and the finest grandson on the planet. From today's perspective, I cannot imagine my life taking a different turn.

Karen and me - 1978

There was a bright light at the end of my tunnel. In the summer of 1976, I couldn't see it.

About 13 years after that motor pool stroll, I was a lieutenant colonel and the commander of a 1,000-man combined arms task force of armor, infantry, and field artillery at Fort Knox. One day, I learned that now-retired Lieutenant General (three-star) Jack Woodmansee was visiting Fort Knox, so I called the protocol office and asked whether he would consider coming to my battalion to discuss leadership with my officers. He agreed and when he arrived, I introduced him by telling my officers about that Friday night in the motor pool years earlier, when I was going through a difficult period.

Leadership is Caring

I recently learned of a story from a graduate course on leadership. On test day, the instructor handed out the exam with only one question: *"What is the name of the janitor who cleans this room?"* Nobody knew, and most thought it a joke.

It wasn't.

Leadership is about reaching out to ALL of those in your sphere of influence and demonstrating that you care about them, personally. The janitor had a role in ensuring the room was adequately cared for, to provide a suitable learning experience for the students. All the students had been exposed to him throughout the course, but nobody had bothered to get to know him or to thank him. But true leadership is in the details of how you care for others.

Nobody passed the test that day, but they all learned a valuable lesson.

Finally, I'm reminded of a Chinese proverb that helps to illustrate that good can come out of bad; that there is usually the possibility of a light at the end of every tunnel.

An old man living out on the Chinese steppes raised horses. One day, his prize stallion ran away. A neighbor felt sorry for him and told him so. The old man replied: *"How could we know it is not a good thing for me?"*

A few days later, the horse returned and brought with it a few mares.

The neighbor congratulated the old man on his good fortune, but the old man replied: *"How could we know it is not a bad thing for me?"*

His son decided to ride one of the horses, but the horse bucked and threw him to the ground, breaking his leg. Again, the neighbor expressed sympathy for the old man, but the old man replied: *"How could we know it is not a good thing for me?"*

A while later the Emperor's army arrived in the area to recruit young men to fight in a war. Because of his crippling injury, the son could not go off to war and was spared from certain death.

This popular Chinese proverb really has a double meaning: that good can come from bad, but also that bad can follow good. The reader can choose what meaning works best for them, but I would point out that there is sometimes a silver lining in misfortune. We just need to have the patience and resolve to find it. There is often light at the end of the tunnel.

There was for me and there can be for you—and those in your charge.

19

What Rocks Are in Your Jar?

"If everything's a priority, then nothing's a priority."
Frank Sonnenberg

Prior to 9/11, I had decided to retire from the Army in 2003 when I reached 30 years in uniform. I announced this decision two years early to give the Army plenty of warning and to allow me to start thinking about getting ready for the next chapter of my life.

When I made this decision, it had been just over a year since my sister's death. A major consideration for me was providing every opportunity to set the conditions for my daughter's launch into life. She had just turned 15, and while there were no indications my ongoing Army career would inhibit her success, I was determined to ensure that she had my full support and the "Dad time" she needed.

I learned of my sister's death when I was on vacation in Hawaii with my family and my parents to ring in the new Millennium. We were at dinner with friends on Christmas Day when the phone rang and my host told me it was the Army Operations Center in the Pentagon, looking for me. When I took the phone, I was told my sister had died, but the circumstances were not yet clear.

We finished our dinner and I asked Karen to take the kids up to our hotel room while I dealt with how to pass this tragic news to my parents. We walked into the grounds of the Hale Koa Hotel in Waikiki and I asked my folks to take a seat at a picnic table under a large monkey pod tree.

My sister with her son Jason, 1993. He became the Marine Chief Warrant Officer who lost his finger on an obstacle course described in Chapter 15.

When I told them that they had just lost their only daughter, my mother fell off the bench and onto the ground. My father sat there in stunned silence, too shocked to speak. Over the next week, we learned that my sister had taken her life for reasons that became more clear only in retrospect. It was too late for us to help her see the "light at the end of her tunnel."

I recently learned of a program run by a retired Marine officer named Mike McNamara called "All Marine Radio." It's an internet-based radio station dedicated to supporting the culture of the Marine Corps and the concept of reducing veteran suicide through greater post-combat related mental health awareness. Its core mission is to help marines deal with stress and trauma by better understanding the criticality and importance of sharing it with others. Their work with the 2ⁿᵈ Marine Division at Camp Lejeune is nothing short of life-saving. Major General Dave Furness, Commanding General of 2ⁿᵈ Marine Division is doing yeoman's work in bringing this difficult subject into the light with the help of Mike McNamara.

There's a reason marines have monikers such as "Devil Dogs" and "Leathernecks." It's because they're among the toughest fighters on the planet. But as I indicated in my Prologue, marines are no different than other people. Underneath that tough outer shell, they have their own challenges in life just like you and me. Culturally, they are less inclined to share it. Mike McNamara and his team are helping to change this. The work that All Marine Radio is doing for the 2ⁿᵈ Marine Division can be applied anywhere and with anyone. I wish that I had been more aware of these principles before I lost my sister 19 years ago. You can learn more about them at allmarineradio.com.

Shortly after I announced my intent to retire, the Army called and asked me to reconsider. I told them I would do whatever the Army Chief of Staff asked, as I had known him for over ten years and had worked for him several times, but if they were asking for my vote, I would like to stay the course with my retirement plans. The next day, they called back and told me the Chief would honor my decision.

When family priorities compete with professional aspirations, you have to decide what's most important.

Filling Your Glass Jar

This next story is another one of many rocks in my backpack that I borrowed from someone else and often pass on. You may have heard it.

A professor is discussing with his class the issue of establishing priorities. He pulls out a large glass jar and a basket of rocks, putting the rocks in the jar until they reach the top. He then asks the class: *"Is the jar full?"* The class answers *"yes."*

He then pulls out a bag of pebbles and pours it in the jar. The pebbles run around the rocks to the bottom of the jar, and when the pebbles reach the top, he asks the class: *"Is the jar full?"* A bit embarrassed, the class responds: *"You fooled us, but yes, the jar is now full."*

He then pulls out a pitcher of water and pours it into the jar. The water finds its way through the rocks and the pebbles and eventually reaches the top rim of the jar. He asks the class: *"Is the jar full?"* The students have now been fooled twice and are a bit gun-shy, but they tentatively say: *"We think so..."*

The professor has nothing else to put in the jar, but tells the class the rocks represent what is most important in life. It could be family, faith, health, their job, a bucket list, money, or climbing the corporate ladder. It doesn't matter. What does matter is that we put the most important rocks in the jar first. If you put water and pebbles in first, not all of the rocks will fit.

A good leader lives this philosophy and encourages his team to do the same. It makes for a more productive and happy organization and even improves your health… through less stress.

Focusing on the Wrong Rocks

He had worked his butt off for over 35 years and the Army had rewarded him with promotions and challenging and demanding assignments, but along the way, his wife left him and now his kids wouldn't talk to him.

A friend of mine graduated from West Point. Long retired as a colonel, he still returned to reunions every year. He once told me he had been to a recent reunion and saw one of his classmates sitting over at the bar, by himself. He wandered over to ask him how he was doing. The classmate turned and my friend saw that he was misty-eyed. He wasn't sure if it was from too many drinks or for some other reason. The classmate—a retired General Officer—then lamented that he had worked his butt off for over 35 years and the Army had rewarded him with promotions and challenging and demanding assignments, but along the way, his wife left him and now his kids wouldn't talk to him.

This is a classic case of an individual struggling to decide what rocks to put in the jar—one that I've seen more than a few times in the military. Throughout his career, the rocks that appear to have been most important to him were associated with career advancement. He was starting to realize that may have been a mistake.

Family First

I have learned in my over 40 of marriage that no matter what I seek to achieve in my career, my family's happiness remains a priority. I related earlier in the book that my first marriage failed, and I subsequently decided that I would not risk losing the woman I loved, nor neglect our children, just to advance my own career. Every decision I made about each promotion I was given or assignment to a new location became an open table discussion that Karen and I would have, and we jointly made the decision together.

I retired from the Army in 2003 and moved to Celebration, Florida—the town that Disney built. My daughter had two years at Celebration High School, then commuted from home to attend the University of Central Florida where she graduated cum laude with a degree in Event Management. She turned a part-time college gig at Disney World into a full-time job after graduation and has advanced through the ranks in the succeeding years. She's happily married, owns her own home, and travels the world. I cannot imagine her life turning out better.

She was the first rock I put in my jar when I retired from the Army in 2003.

When my daughter was approaching graduation from college, Karen indicated a desire to move back to Hawaii. I agreed and I started to look for opportunities there. As you've learned from a previous chapter, the Marine Corps created a senior level position there in late 2009. I applied, was accepted, and we moved back to the islands in the summer of 2010. The past nine years have been a wonderful experience, as my son was already living in Hawaii, got married, and they gave us a grandson. He and his wife—with my 3-year old grandson—have since moved to Japan.

In mid-2018, Karen again indicated a desire to turn the page—this time to the east coast to be closer to her large family (including our daughter). At this writing, we're preparing to move to Bluffton, South Carolina for the next chapter of our life.

I've learned what rocks to put in my jar… and when. You should too.

20

Remember Your Roots

"Humility is not thinking less of yourself,
it's thinking of yourself less."

C.S. Lewis

I continually remind myself as a retired General Officer and senior executive that at one time in my life, I was no different from anyone who works for me today. I have walked in their shoes, worked hard, and followed the orders and guidance of someone above me. I contributed to the effectiveness of the whole and—at times—my efforts contributed to successes. The fact that I recognize that the next generation is now doing what I once did is something that I like to think keeps me humble, and the people around me more comfortable.

I was reminded of this a few years ago when I was on a Navy ship at sea. In addition to my primary duties as the Deputy Commanding General of the Army in the Pacific, I held a collateral duty as the Chief of Staff for a four-star, Navy-led Joint Task Force. This involved exercises at sea on the USS Blue Ridge, the command ship for 7th Fleet, based in Yokosuka, Japan. I first worked for Admiral Tom Fargo, then Admiral Walt Doran.

When I boarded the Blue Ridge in 2002, Vice Admiral Robert "Rat" Willard, the 7th Fleet Commander, gave up his state room just across from Admiral Doran, my boss. Willard was a CAPSTONE classmate of mine who later became the Vice Chief of Naval Operations and then Commander of U.S. Pacific Command. An F14 pilot, he performed aerial stunts in the movie *Top Gun*.

By Army standards, the stateroom was palatial. It included a bedroom, a conference room, and a separate "head" (bathroom). To me, it was the Navy equivalent of a suite in a 5-star hotel and was close enough to the Officers Mess that I could smell bread baking every morning when I awoke. Several times a week, they would have "make your own ice cream sundae" night—open at 10 p.m. Contrasting that to much of my time in the Army—where I spent many nights in the heat or cold either on a cot or on the front fender of my tank—I was in heaven.

Before we left port, the Command Master Chief (senior enlisted advisor to the ship's captain) came by to check on me. He asked: *"How are we taking care of you, sir?"* I replied: *"Had I known it would be like this, I might have joined the Navy decades ago."* He assured me that if I had joined the Navy 30 years ago, I wouldn't have started off like this. He then offered a tour of the ship.

We started at the very bottom of the ship, near the keel. There, I saw sailors chipping rust off the interior hull with a chisel and hammer. We then passed through the engine room, which was extremely hot and noisy, and we wound our way up through a berthing area, where I saw the closet-like living spaces afforded each sailor. I gained a greater appreciation for the average sailor's life that day, and it only grew in the days to come.

We pulled out of port, traversed Tokyo Bay, and headed into the Western Pacific. Unbeknownst to me, there was a growing storm forming south of Guam. It would become the third strongest typhoon to hit Guam in recorded history, after one in 1900 and another in 1962.

At its peak, *Typhoon Pongsona* had sustained winds of 144 mph with gusts to 173 mph. When it hit Guam on the 8th of December, 2002, it knocked out communications, damaging 715 power poles and 513 transformers. Anemometers along the northern coast failed from the winds, and the Guam Memorial Hospital had several walls collapse. *Pongsona* left 65% of the island's water wells inoperable and destroyed or damaged 1,300 homes. With almost 26" of rainfall in a short time frame, flooding occurred across the island, and the storm surge reached 20 feet at some locations.

The typhoon injured 193 people, mostly from lacerations and fractures caused by flying debris and glass. One victim suffered a fatal heart attack and medical help couldn't reach her in time to render aid.

Back on the USS Blue Ridge, the captain realized we were in the path of *Pongsona* so he turned the ship around and headed back to Tokyo Bay to ride it out. The next 24 hours were among the most miserable I've experienced. While we were not directly in the typhoon, we were close enough to feel its strong effects. The Navy doesn't build ships for comfort or smooth sailing; they're built for efficiency and war-fighting. One of the features that differentiates them from cruise ships is that many have flat bottoms to help them navigate shallow waters. But this makes them bounce like corks in stormy weather. The Blue Ridge was doing exactly that as we headed back to Tokyo Bay.

Few on the ship escaped seasickness, including one of my main staff officers, Brigadier General Chuck Jacoby, who later became a four-star general and commander of Northern Command—the command that was established after 9/11 and charged with protecting the United States homeland against attack. When I saw how miserable Chuck was feeling, I encouraged him to join me up on the deck where we could see the horizon and feel the wind in our face; much preferable to bouncing around in a stateroom down below.

*Chuck Jacoby and I getting some fresh air during
the escape from Typhoon Pongsona - 2002*

On reflection, I am now glad I joined the Army 30 years prior, as I'm not sure my stomach could have handled decades of churn like I experienced that day. It gave me a greater appreciation for what my Navy brethren go through when deployed.

But, back to the main point of this chapter.

I also gained a great appreciation for the contribution of the Blue Ridge's crew in getting us where we needed to go safely and efficiently, and allowing us to conduct the training exercise using their ship as our classroom.

> *I wanted to ensure this Army General made clear my appreciation to the sailors on the Blue Ridge. I did this with an oft-used leadership technique called "LBWA" or Leadership-By-Walking-Around.*

I wanted to ensure this *Army* General made clear my appreciation to the sailors on the Blue Ridge. I did this with an oft-used leadership technique called "LBWA" or Leadership-By-Walking-Around. Whenever I was able to break free from the training exercise on the ship, which I did at least once a day, I roamed the decks and told sailors how much I appreciated what they were doing for us. I have used LBWA throughout my Army career, as well, especially when I became a General Officer. I have always tried to show my appreciation for those in my organization.

When I was a battalion commander, commanding 1,000 soldiers, I told all my leaders that every one of their troopers would be welcome to join my family *in my home* on Christmas Day if they had no place to go. Over half the soldiers in the battalion were single, and I didn't want any of them sitting in the barracks feeling sorry for themselves. I never needed to host a soldier, as my leaders were adequately incentivized to ensure each of their soldiers were taken care of on that special day. That may have been the case all along, but my open-door invitation likely assured it.

Another way to show your appreciation is through "spot recognition." Since at least the mid-1980s, the military has had a custom whereby commanders—particularly at the lieutenant colonel rank and above—carry "challenge coins" with them when they visit the troops. These coins are typically customized to the position the senior official serves in, with his or her organizational seal or emblem emblazoned on one side and the rank of the official on the other.

I've had these coins since I was a lieutenant colonel commander at Fort Knox. They're called "challenge coins" because once they are given to someone, the presenter tells the recipient that if they run into each other in the future, they can "challenge" each other on whether they have the coin in their possession. If one doesn't, he or she owes the other a drink.

They are presented as "on the spot" recognition for good work. Some servicemembers prize these coins more than medals and try to get as many as they can.

Challenge coins are typically paid for with taxpayer dollars. As such, there are strict rules on who they can be given to and for what purpose. However, since I became a General Officer, I have purchased my own so as not to be bound by these rules. Over the years, I've passed out thousands of coins, and I always tried to target those people who work where the rubber meets the road: junior-level soldiers, sailors, airmen, marines, or civilian employees.

Frederick Smith, Founder, Chairman and CEO of FedEx Corporation wrote in a 2008 U.S. Naval Institute *"Proceedings"* article the following:

> *"...I've also incorporated Marine Corps tenets into FedEx. If you were to drop in on one of our management training seminars, you'd recognize from your military days what's being taught. We tell our executives that the key to their success is to rely on their first-level managers (FedEx's counterparts of NCOs); to set an example themselves; and to praise in public when someone has done a good job. All these are standard operating procedures in the Marines. But they're a rarity in the industrial world.*
>
> *In the Navy, a ship's captain flies Bravo and Zulu signal flags when his crew has done a good job. Our FedEx managers affix a sticker with BZ pennants on it to reports from subordinates that are particularly good. Workers who excel get to wear a BZ lapel pin, adorned with Bravo and Zulu flags. When an employee goes out of his way for a customer, he gets a "BZ check" of $150 - $200. Except for bonuses, these practices come straight out of the Marine Corps Leadership Manuals..."*

It is those who follow you who helped you get where you are and keep you on top of the mountain.

When you rise to become a leader—particularly a senior-level leader—never forget your roots. Always remember that *it is those who follow you who helped you get where you are and keep you on top of the mountain.*

Recognize their contributions frequently and you will be amazed at what they will give you back in return.

21

When Multi-Level Marketing Works

"An entrepreneur with strong networks
makes money even when he is asleep."

Amit Kalantri

Readers in the business world know all about multi-level marketing (MLM) – a sales technique used to sell products and services in companies like Avon, Amway, Mary Kay Cosmetics, Tupperware, and Legal Shield. You may have a positive or a negative view of MLM, depending on your experience (or lack thereof) with them. Whatever your view, it may surprise you to know that the U.S. Army has used similar techniques to support an important cause.

Here's the story.

After running a national conference on Information Sharing and Homeland Security for three years, from 2004-2006, I remained on the Board of Advisors of the National Conference Services, Inc. and attended their advisory board meetings in Maryland twice a year.

In January of 2008, I had just completed one such meeting and was walking through a blizzard to my rental car to get back to Baltimore's airport and then the warmth of Florida. My phone rang as I was scraping ice off the window, and it was Brigadier General John "J.J." Johnson, a great Army leader who had taken my job as commander of the Army's Community and Family Support Center five years after I left the Army.

I knew J.J. because I was the retiree representative on the Army's Morale, Welfare, and Recreation Board of Directors. I saw him periodically at board meetings. He told me that the Secretary of the Army, Pete Geren, wanted to start a new program that provided opportunities for the American public to recognize the service and sacrifices of soldiers and their families, and for them to be able to demonstrate that support through both word and deed.

He called it "Community Covenant."

Secretary Geren believed Americans were becoming numb to the sacrifices of soldiers and their families now entering the 7th year of the global war on terrorism. He was concerned that this ambivalence not turn negatively on the military in the way public opposition to the Vietnam War did. He wanted to "reconnect the American people to our nation's Army."

The only way I could reach every corner of America in a short period of time was to network into like-minded organizations that could help me carry the message and implement the program.

J.J. asked if I would be interested in coming to D.C. for about 6 months to get this effort "jump-started." I could then turn it back to Army staff.

Within weeks, I had rented an apartment in Crystal City, Virginia and was off and running.

What happened next is where the MLMs come into play. I had learned from a friend in Tampa about some successful multi-level marketing (MLM) techniques with a company now called Legal Shield and decided to apply that methodology to access the American public as quickly as possible.

I knew that the only way I could reach every corner of America in a short period of time was to network into like-minded organizations that could help me carry the message and implement the program.

I started inside the Army with the "Civilian Aides to the Secretary of the Army," the Army's "Reserve Ambassadors," the U.S. Army Recruiting Command, the Reserve Officers Training Corps (ROTC), the National Guard, and the Army Reserve. These organizations are represented in every state and territory. I then branched out to veteran organizations: The American Legion, Veterans of Foreign Wars, and Disabled American Veterans (DAV). Finally, I started reaching out to other organizations such as the League of Cities.

Like the pied piper, I traveled all over the country, speaking to various groups. The MLM part of it was that I asked each national group to sign a Covenant, and then encourage their local chapters to do the same, in support of our Army. This pyramiding of efforts would thereby foster a broad new level of support through demonstrative words, plus the provision of tangible programs and resources in support of our troops.

It wasn't long before I learned that the American public clearly cared about our Army, but they obviously also cared about the other services: marines, airmen, and sailors.

I recommended to Secretary Geren that we broaden our effort to include the entire military. He agreed, and from that point forward—while I was working for the Army—I was also representing the interests of all military Services.

After 6 months, we had developed strong momentum. Ultimately, every governor in the country and hundreds of cities, towns, and counties had signed Covenants, with many pledging what ultimately resulted in millions of dollars of support to our troops, in various ways.

Approaching the end of my 6-month commitment, I was asked to extend another two months to carry it through the Association of the United States Army (AUSA) Symposium, conducted annually in October of each year in Washington D.C. I agreed.

When Secretary Geren spoke at the Symposium, he pulled me out of the audience to recognize me for the work I had done on Community Covenant. He pinned a Meritorious Civilian Service Award medal on my chest, the second highest award given to civilian employees. I was humbled by this recognition, but glad that I had made a difference on behalf of our servicemembers and their families.

Secretary Geren recognizing me at the Association of United States Army (AUSA) annual symposium - 2008

The next day, I was getting ready to head back to Florida when Secretary Geren's Executive Officer called and asked me to come to the Pentagon so the Secretary could say goodbye. When I entered his office, another small ceremony followed, with Mr. Geren pinning the Decoration for Exceptional Civilian Service medal on my chest. Puzzled, I asked him why we were doing this twice, in two days, with two different medals. He responded, *"Yesterday's medal was from the Army; this one is from me."*

I later learned that he had wanted to present me with the top award at the AUSA Symposium, but Army policy requires that the recipient first be the holder of the lower-level medal before being eligible for the top one.

He then asked if I would stay on the program longer. I told him that with the momentum we had, I could continue as a consultant, working from my home in Florida. He agreed, and within a month or two, I had a signed contract with the Army and was off to the races for another year. My two years with Community Covenant were among the most satisfying experiences I've ever had.

MLM companies are not all that different than what we see going on with social media these days, where someone posts and shares a piece of news, their friends then share it to their tribe, and friends of their friends then share it further.

Just like a video can go viral on YouTube, so can a good idea.

If you are involved in any type of marketing or promotion for your organization from your leadership perch, the point of this story is that you should be open to any techniques that work to get people talking and responding in a positive way.

When you want to create change or draw attention to a positive cause, think MLM.

22

Having a Plan B...

"Hope is Not a Method."
General Gordon Sullivan,
32nd Chief of Staff, U.S. Army

In 2007, I was asked to speak at the All-American Bowl—an annual high school all-star football game in San Antonio, Texas sponsored by Army Recruiting Command. This event brings together the best players in the country from East and West. They wanted me to speak to parents about their sons having a "Plan B."

Athletes at this level believe they are destined for greatness. They want to be the next Tom Brady, Patrick Mahomes, Aaron Donald, or Ezekiel Elliot. Most of them are severely disappointed when it does not happen. In my talk to the parents, I focused on the single digit statistics of making it to the professional level, and I knew I needed to reach those who were unbelievers.

I also had to walk the tightrope of bringing such reality to their attention without discouraging their sons from "climbing their own mountain." Even if the talent is there, injury could sideline them for life. This has happened many times.

To this audience, I spoke about the risks of putting all the eggs in this one "football" basket and having no back-up plan. Just about every player there was headed to a full-ride college scholarship on the merits of their athletic skills, but the majority of them would not make it to the pros—either because their talent fell just short, or because of an injury sustained in college, which they couldn't yet foresee.

Plan B was about having a back-up plan if Plan A didn't pan out.

Plan B was about having a back-up plan if Plan A didn't pan out. I suggested that everyone develop a second skill set—other than football—that they could focus on when they weren't on the playing field. This might include considering ROTC and an Army career.

I'm not sure I reached every parent, but several of them came up to me afterwards to thank me for *"sprinkling around some reality dust"* and helping them to give their kids the appropriate warning and preparation.

A few years later, I spoke at a venue in Jacksonville, Florida which had former pro-football players participating as well. One morning, I had breakfast with a retired eight-year All-Pro center from the New York Giants who told me that when he was recruited—and before he had even given the first snap of his rookie year—the scout that recruited him said: *"It's my job to find your replacement."* That was a sobering moment for this fellow, particularly since he had not yet played in his first professional game.

The NFL is a monopoly. With the exception of the Canadian Football League, there are few options for those who aspire to play professionally. He told me that a player gets "vested for retirement" only after playing just a few years. If they are not under contract the following year, they are out on the street, usually in their mid-twenties. The majority of players never make it past this threshold.

My point to the parents in San Antonio that day was that—no

matter the level of talent they currently had—their sons need a "Plan B" in case they reach 25 years old with nowhere to go.

As I indicated in Chapter 10, they should strive to reach an achievable rung on their ladder, but have another ladder nearby.

23

Leaving a Legacy

"The true meaning of life is to plant trees,
under whose shade you do not expect to sit."

Nelson Henderson

Every high-level executive yearns to leave an imprint on the future of his or her organization. It is only natural that one wants to create something meaningful and lasting that everyone will appreciate and look up to after your time is over. Knowing that you have contributed to your organization leaves you feeling proud of your work, your commitment, and the investment you've made in your job. And, if you are able to create at least one legacy while you are still on the job, it can make you an even better leader, eager to continue making more contributions during the remainder of your years in executive positions. But more important than doing it for yourself, you should do it for the betterment of the organization.

After my 22 months in the Pentagon in the late 90s, I returned to the Army, this time as the Commander of the Army's Community and Family Support Center. This was the organization that oversaw the $1.6 billion business of providing morale, welfare, and recreation programs in support of soldiers and their families. My headquarters was fortunately in Alexandria, Virginia, so I didn't need to uproot my family again. The Army thought I was a natural fit for this position, since I had recently commanded a base and delivered such services at the retail level.

I quickly discovered several major projects that had to get done, that would improve the quality of life of our soldiers and their families. One of these was Army fitness centers where soldiers and their families could work out in their off hours.

It was clear that our fitness centers were a poster child for how the Army might have been falling short in taking care of its troops. Regrettably, we had too many gyms in the Army at that time that were large buildings with no air conditioning, a few basketball courts, medicine balls in the corner, gang latrines and showers that were often plugged, and manned by soldiers waiting to be discharged for drugs or other misconduct.

I'm exaggerating a bit…but not by much.

I set about to fix this, not to the standards of Gold's Gym, but at least to YMCA standards—a standard the American people should expect us to provide our soldiers, who have a "contractual obligation" to stay fit. I testified before Congressional committees for more resources because many of the fitness facilities necessary to ensure we had a fit Army were falling short. We convinced Congress that by establishing standards, and quantifiably measuring those standards, we could identify resourcing shortfalls to fix it. Doing this, we were able to get increased funding, and today's fitness centers on Army installations are something to be proud of.

Another initiative we spearheaded was to establish public-private ventures that used commercial developer investments, not taxpayer dollars. We launched our first venture with a car wash at Fort Carson, Colorado in 1999 and today we have millions of corporate dollars (rather than taxpayer dollars) invested in programs and services to support soldiers and their families.

Another legacy left was the upgrade of four world-class Armed Forces Recreation Centers. Among these were several hotels near the Austrian Alps in Garmisch, Germany; a hotel at Disney World in Orlando, Florida; another on Waikiki Beach in Honolulu, Hawaii; and a hotel in Seoul, Korea. These venues serve servicemembers, retirees, and their families when on vacation or traveling in those regions.

We had two issues with these properties on my arrival in 1998. In Germany, nestled in the Bavarian Alps, we operated multiple pre-World War II hotels that were outdated, expensive to run, and small. We were losing over $1M per year because of their inefficient operations and decaying infrastructure. At Disney World, we had purchased their golf resort hotel in the mid-1980s, and renamed it *"Shades of Green."* It was bursting at the seams from the demand and was among the highest occupancy hotels in the resort industry. Servicemembers needed reservations almost a year in advance. It was simply too small.

With the support of Congressman John McHugh (later Secretary of the Army), I convinced senior Army leadership to allow the return of the German hotels to Germany, and then to acquire commercial financing of $145,000,000 to construct a new hotel in Germany and double the size of our hotel at Disney World. All this could be done without spending tax dollars and could be repaid over a 30-year period from revenues generated from the properties.

One of the important considerations that took the proposal over the finish line with General Shinseki—then Chief of Staff of the Army—was the ability to improve our force protection posture at the Germany-based properties. It had been just over two years since the Khobar Towers bombing in Saudi Arabia and the vulnerability of our troops to further terrorist attack was obvious. Most of the hotels in Germany were separated from a potential attacker by little more than the width of a sidewalk. With our proposal, we had the ability to design, relocate, and build a new property that didn't sit just feet from a public road, thereby dramatically improving our protection posture.

Our plan was ultimately approved, and today we have a wonderful hotel inside a military base in Garmisch, Germany named *Edelweiss.* The *Shades of Green* hotel in Florida has doubled its capacity and added conferencing capabilities. And, the thirty-year commercial loan is being paid back by the revenues generated by the wonderful facilities' use—not taxpayer dollars.

Ironically, because the construction of the hotel in Germany occurred after my departure to my next assignment, I've never seen it. But because I retired from the Army in 2003 and moved to Celebration, Florida near Disney World, I was able to attend the ribbon cutting for the expansion of the *Shades of Green.*

"...let your greatest legacy be that you pass on the best-of-breed leadership traits you've learned from others."

What is the legacy you wish to leave to the future in your organization? Are you on the way to accomplishing it? What are the challenges you face to get it implemented? Are you being selfless in wanting to see it done? Are you doing these things for the right reasons? These are all good questions to ponder about your own leadership legacy.

But as I said at the end of Chapter 3, if nothing else, *"...let your greatest legacy be that you pass on the best-of-breed leadership traits you've learned from others."*

24

The Buck Stops Where?

"The buck stops here..."
President Harry Truman

In my many years of experience in the military and in civilian leadership roles, I have always abided by the philosophy that I "owned" decisions that I made. If something went right, I credited the team that helped us achieve that milestone, but if something went wrong, it belonged to me. I effectively adopted the well-known phrase of President Truman, who rightly said of his presidency, *"The Buck Stops Here."*

Leaders should admit to and address their mistakes. In most instances, if the mistake has not threatened lives or caused substantial harm, a leader who made a mistake should be given another chance to fix the problem and carry on in his leadership role.

In the 1980s, the U.S. military introduced a system for evaluating training called the "After Action Review" or AAR. After a major training event, a unit would reflect on what went well and what didn't go so well, and the session would often be kicked off by the leader stepping up to admit the mistakes *he* made. It was one of the many tools that helped us distance ourselves from a "zero-defects" environment which many felt we were in at that point in time. It also quickly became something that separated us from many of the militaries around the world.

If people are hesitant to acknowledge what went wrong, there is less chance of fixing it. And, by leaders being self-critical, it makes it easier for the rest of the team to follow their lead. AARs helped make us a better military, and have survived and thrived for decades. They are now used in everyday operations in the military and, like the Military Decision-Making Process (MDMP) discussed in Chapter 8, they have become second nature and are often used in our personal lives as well.

In some instances, however, it may be that the mistake has caused harm, jeopardized lives, lost money, or contributed to significant chaos in the organization. When this occurs, the leader should take responsibility and may need to suffer the consequences, losing his or her job.

Taking a strict stand on mistakes, however, can lead to a conundrum for many people. What if the leader has always excelled in every prior decision? What if the leader is highly respected by every person he or she has ever worked with? What if there are actual mitigating reasons for the leader's mistake? What if there are deep-rooted errors in the system that the leader has not yet had time to fix? These are all considerations that should be addressed before taking irreversible action on the leader's role and future.

Consider the following case and think about what you would do.

The situation involves the inbound missile warning system in Hawaii that many readers may recall was inadvertently activated in early 2018.

I was familiar with the state's civil defense system because I had been hired after my retirement from the Army to return to Hawaii and consult on some disaster response exercises. During these exercises, I shadowed Major General Vern Miyagi, someone I had known from my time in Hawaii as Deputy Commander of U.S. Army Pacific. He had a key position in the state Civil Defense.

Years later, when I returned to work for the Marine Corps, I ran across Vern. He had retired from the National Guard and was now the civilian head of Hawaii's state Civil Defense.

On January 12, 2018, I was attending a luncheon at the Hawaii Governor's mansion. Sitting across the table from me was Vern. Making small talk, I joked, *"Vern, I just want you to know how well I sleep at night, knowing you're protecting us from attack."* He laughed and we went on with the lunch.

Twenty hours later, Hawaii mistakenly issued a state-wide alert that a ballistic missile was inbound—presumably from North Korea. It took 38 minutes before we received a second message indicating the first alert was a false alarm. People across Hawaii were rattled and the state was embarrassed. It became a national story; perhaps international.

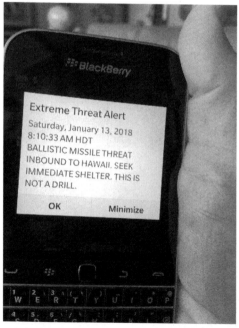

"Inbound missile" alert in Hawaii - 13 January 2018

The Governor's opponent in the upcoming election made a big deal about this mistake, citing the personal responsibility of the Governor.

In the aftermath of this false alarm, Vern publicly took responsibility and lost his job. The Governor was re-elected.

> *In the aftermath of this false alarm, Vern publicly took responsibility and lost his job. The Governor was re-elected.*

It was a sad day to see Vern lose his job over this event. Vern Miyagi was, and remains, a great public servant and a class act for the way he stepped up and took full responsibility when he knew what would follow—the loss of his livelihood.

How would you act in this situation? Would you have accepted responsibility as Vern did? Did the buck really stop at his desk? It's a tough call, no doubt, but one we all should ponder if we're to be great leaders.

Epilogue

Saving Private Ryan

To open this book, I wrote about the legacy of my father's service in India and China during World War II. That was a *true* story. To close this book, let me relate to you a *fictional* story; one that still has its roots in World War II, but this time in Europe. I often tell this story when speaking to groups.

Most readers have seen the film *Saving Private Ryan*, starring Tom Hanks as Captain John Miller and Matt Damon as Private Ryan. It's the story of four brothers who go off to war. Three are killed in combat and the Chief of Staff of the Army decides that their mother must not lose her sole surviving son. He orders a mission to go find Private Ryan and bring him back.

Captain Miller (Tom Hanks) leads a small group of soldiers behind enemy lines to find and return Private Ryan. Several in his patrol are killed along the way, but Miller eventually finds Private Ryan with a small group of 101st Airborne soldiers, guarding a bridge against a much larger and more powerful German force. He tells Ryan of his brothers' deaths and that his orders are to bring him home.

Private Ryan refuses.

"What are we supposed to tell your mother?" Miller asks.

"Tell her I was here. Tell her I'm with the only brothers I have left. There's no way I'm going to leave this bridge," Ryan responds.

Captain Miller tells Private Ryan of the death of his three brothers
(Photo reproduced with permission. © Paramount Pictures)

If you've seen the movie, you know that Captain Miller dies on that bridge. Before he does, he whispers into Ryan's ear, *"Earn this ... earn it."*

He was telling Ryan not to let his—nor his men's ultimate sacrifice—go without purpose. He was telling Ryan to *lead a purposeful life.*

The movie then flashes forward about 50 years and we find Private Ryan—now an old man—standing over Captain Miller's grave. With tears in his eyes, he stands, salutes, then turns to his wife and says, *"Tell me I've led a good life. Tell me I'm a good man."*

While Tom Brokaw once called World War II Americans—my father's era—*The Greatest Generation,* today's warriors are equal to the honor. After the longest continuous period of combat in our nation's history, we still see young men and women step forward and say, *"Send me!"*

Soldiers, sailors, airmen and marines. Time and time again. Do not lose faith in young people. I am humbled to have spent time in their ranks and look forward to supporting the next *greatest generation* in my sunset years. I hope you do, too.

Finally, as I said in the prologue, over the past 50 years I've experienced both good and bad leaders, doing my best to learn from both. It remains a journey, not a destination, as learning never stops. This book is intended to pass on to others what I've learned along the way.

Take what you want. Discard what you don't.

Then pay it forward...

Army Strong and Semper Fi!

Appendix A

Whelden Philosophy of Command

Department of the Army
Headquarters, 2nd Battalion, 10th Cavalry
194th Armored Brigade (Sep)
Fort Knox, Kentucky 40121

AFVL-AR-CO
27 July 1989

MEMORANDUM FOR Leaders of 2nd Bn, 10th Cavalry

SUBJECT: My Philosophy of Command

1. As I join the 2nd Bn, 10th Cavalry, I owe it to each of you to describe, in some detail, my philosophy of command. These basic beliefs and values have developed and grown throughout my 16 years in the Army. They have been influenced by my family, my peers, and a number of senior officers and NCOs with whom I have served. They will help you understand what I believe is important, what is less consequential, and what is

non-negotiable. If you understand the thrust of this memo, you will understand me.

a. **Safety.** Nothing is more important than the safety and well-being of our soldiers and their families. Leaders must constantly be alert in the training environment. They must lead by example, in order to recognize symptoms of unsafe conditions: heat and cold injuries, soldier fatigue and inattentiveness, sleep plans in the field, etc.

Leaders must all understand the principle of risk management. It is an assessment process involving a few simple steps to determine if the benefits of taking a risk outweigh the possible cost of the risk. Leaders who do not understand or practice this process must get on board ASAP.

We must not forget the potential risks for soldiers when off-duty. Regular briefings and discussions about off-duty hazards should be frequent, detailed, and should reach every soldier.

b. **Care of Soldiers.** Our most valuable resource is the soldiers we lead. They are the critical link in everything we do, and deserve the best training and leadership we can offer. Soldiers expect confident, capable leaders. I expect officers and NCOs to lead by example, to treat soldiers with dignity and respect, and to demand the same in return. If a soldier is not producing, we owe it to the Army to remove him. If a leader is not producing, we owe it to our soldiers to remove him. Take care of your soldiers and you will quickly see the benefits. Abuse him and you will see me.

c. **Role of the NCO.** It has been said that the NCO is the "Backbone of the Army." I believe this. No other individual plays as critical a role in mission accomplishment. The NCO is at the cutting edge of training, maintenance, leading, and caring.

When a specialist becomes a sergeant, he enters a whole new world. His scope of responsibility expands dramatically, and he should be justly proud of this new level of achievement and stature. His entrance into the NCO Corps is a rite of passage which should be hosted by the other NCOs in his unit.

NCOs should lead their soldiers rather than direct them. When I see soldiers in the motor pool or at a training site, their sergeant should be with them. He is responsible for their individual and crew training, their appearance, and the condition of their clothing, equipment, and living area. He is responsible for their safety, on and off duty. He is available anytime of the day or night to ensure the well-being of the soldiers he leads.

Good NCOs take great pride in the condition of their equipment, and the training and welfare of their men. They are intolerant of those few who abuse their equipment or their men. Such performance insults the fine traditions and professionalism of the NCO Corps. The outstanding NCO doesn't need to brag; his troops will do it for him.

I have great respect for the NCO Corps. I would not have had this privilege to command without the professionalism and dedicated support of NCOs like yourselves. You can make this the finest tank battalion in the Army – one that soldiers, officers, and other NCOs will be proud to join – let's do it together.

d. **Role of the Staff.** Your role is to serve the battalion and its subordinate troops. Although it may be difficult to see from your perspective, the synchronization between your staff section, others in the battalion, and your counterpart at brigade, is absolutely critical. Don't wait until then; begin synchronizing your efforts now. The XO will help you.

Don't bring an action to me without having done thorough staff work. This means defining the problem, identifying and comparing the courses of action available, and making a recommendation. Run it through the XO first. Don't expect to leave the action with me – I will not do your staff work. When you leave my office, you should take the action with you: either with a decision or guidance. Staff actions within the battalion can be handwritten or verbal if concise, legible, and permitted by regulation. Staff actions or correspondence external to the battalion (except informal intra-staff correspondence) will be first class and seen by me.

Be a team player. As a general rule, you should not challenge guidance or tasks from brigade. Let the XO or myself do that. The same is true in your dealings with troop commanders. If you find a problem with a troop in your staff area, discuss it with the troop commander first. If he fails to respond, then bring it to the attention of the XO. Avoid developing the "we-they" syndrome so often found in dysfunctional units. We are a team, and I evaluate all of you on your ability to foster that spirit.

Staff work is often tedious, boring, and time-consuming. It is much more fun to be a commander, and they seem to get all the recognition. I understand the vital importance of your (often, behind-the-scenes) work in the overall accomplishment of the battalion's mission. I have been there. Your long hours, hard work, and commitment will not go unnoticed.

e. **Role of the XO.** The executive officer is my second-in-command (2IC) and the chief of staff. Generally, he will give guidance and directives to the staff, whereas I will speak directly to troop commanders. However, in my absence, he speaks for me, and I expect both staff and commanders to respond accordingly. If you, as a commander, disagree with his directives, you have the right to bring it to my attention. Meanwhile, follow his orders.

The XO will rate all primary and special staff, except the S3 who will work directly for me. This does not mean, however, that the S3 bypasses the XO in training and operational matters. Part of his evaluation is his ability to coordinate and synchronize with the XO and the rest of the staff.

The XO is responsible for training the staff. In the field, he will be the "battle captain" and will synchronize all combat, combat support, and combat service support from the task force Tactical Operations Center (TOC).

f. **Role of the CSM.** The Command Sergeant Major is responsible to me alone. He is my primary implementor of all enlisted actions. He has the freedom to go anywhere in the battalion area, and often will. He will be visible in the motor pool, in training areas, and in the field.

I expect him to feel the pulse of the battalion, to understand my standards, objectives, and priorities, and to see that they are implemented through the NCO chain of command. I expect him to do this in a manner which does not cut across the traditional chain of command, isolating troop commanders. I expect him to lead by example in all areas: PT, NCOPD, maintenance, and training.

He will closely manage individual soldier training, weapons qualification, physical fitness training, enlisted promotions, schooling and assignments, in-processing, and the welcoming of new soldiers and their families. In addition, he will monitor MOS shortages, actively participate in enlisted UCJM actions, conduct promotion boards, monitor SEERs, and provide advice and counsel to battalion staff and troop commanders as needed. He is the keeper of the battalion colors and will ensure that ceremonies are conducted properly.

g. **Training**. The late Bear Bryant once said: "The team that blocks and tackles the best usually wins the game." The principle applies equally well to our task of training for combat. The key to success is mastery of individual and collective skills at platoon level and below.

Through our battle focus, we will identify the absolute critical individual METL tasks from the SQT, crew drills from FM 17-12-1 and the MTP, and the TE&Os from the MTP which support our troop METL. These skills will be practiced and practiced. Concurrently, we will train troop commanders and the staff in the skills necessary to synchronize this effort at troop and task force level.

Training should be well-planned, innovative, and fun. It should focus on identified weaknesses, and should challenge soldiers. In most cases, standards are already established in appropriate MTPs, FMs, or Soldier Manuals. Where they are not, we will establish standards. In some cases, we will raise the standard to challenge our soldiers even more.

Leaders must understand the crawl, walk, run principle and use it appropriately. An over-resourced and extravagant training event will have negative results if it is too complicated for your troops.

Learn how to conduct proper After Action Reviews (AARs) and use them at every training event. The learning from these sessions sometimes exceeds the event itself.

Finally, don't waste soldiers' time. If you finish early, move onto something else. If some soldiers achieve ahead of others, give them something else to do, or give them some time off.

h. **Maintenance**. Training and maintenance are almost inseparable in an armor battalion. Although maintenance isn't as exciting as training, it can certainly be as challenging and is no less important.

I hold vehicle commanders primarily responsible for the status of their vehicles and the chain of command for checking that status. Just as a well-trained crew is a source of pride, so should be the continuous operational status of that crew's vehicle.

When I ask about the status of your vehicle, don't tell me *"It's on my 2404;" "I reported it to the Motor Sergeant;"* or *"It's been like that since I was assigned to it."* Those are what I call non-answers, and they will raise my blood pressure (and yours). Tell me what <u>YOU</u> are doing to fix it. There may be extenuating circumstances which you don't control, but let's not start our discussion by stumbling through those. Tell me up front what's wrong and what's being done to fix it. That's what I want to hear.

I will provide more guidance in the area of maintenance after assessing the status and condition of our vehicles and equipment.

i. **BE GOOD, LOOK GOOD**. It took me a long time to learn the importance of appearances. I used to believe that if my troops and equipment were capable of performing their wartime mission (and I knew that), then it didn't really matter what others deduced from what they saw. I was dead wrong. If your motor pool line is sloppy at the end of the day, or tarps are haphazardly tied down; if your bay areas are disheveled and oil spills are not properly picked up; if your bumper markings are sloppy or your soldiers aren't sharp at morning formation, then you will give a poor impression to those outside the battalion. You will also give a poor impression to those inside the battalion.

I remember an incident on REFORGER a few years ago when a unit was moving towards the FEBA and was being observed by a number of general officers visiting from CONUS. External stowage on the tanks was not uniform, tarps were flapping, and crew members were not all in the same headgear. The generals carried back the impression that it was a sloppy, undisciplined unit. It didn't matter (and they didn't know) that this unit saved the division that day because of its tactical skills and responsiveness.

BE GOOD, LOOK GOOD. Soldiers appreciation a sharp, clean, organized work environment. It is infectious and will improve their performance. It reflects discipline and pride. It makes us all feel good about ourselves and our unit.

One caution: This does NOT mean painting over rust spots in the hope that that the rust will go away, or cleaning up oil spills by just covering them up. It also does not mean putting soldiers through unnecessary make-work just for appearance's sake. This battalion will not build its reputation at the expense of its soldiers. It is possible to both Be Good and Look Good. Make it a habit – you and your soldiers will both appreciate the effort.

j. **Physical Fitness**. I am not a PT fanatic. However, I do believe that every soldier regardless of age, rank, or MOS should maintain a certain level of fitness. This means that he should be able to pass the APFT at any time while striving to score above 240. He should be capable of meeting the Corps standard of 4 miles in 36 minutes. He should not exceed the Army's weight control standard or even have the appearance of being overweight.

Physical fitness training will be conducted primarily at troop level and below, and will focus on improving cardiovascular fitness, muscular strength, and endurance. This means that achieving standards will require commanders to depart from a "daily dozen and unit run" mentality and be much more innovative and tailored in their approach. Soldiers have differing abilities and must be challenged at different levels. The objective is not for all soldiers to reach the same minimum level of fitness, but rather, for each soldier to maximize his own potential.

Battalion runs will occur once per month, will average 3-4 miles, and will be conducted at a 9 minute/mile pace. The purpose of these runs will be to foster cohesion and spirit within the battalion. In addition, they will meet the Corps requirement of 4 miles in 36 minutes. More to come.

k. **Awards**. We all appreciate being recognized for good performance. I believe all soldiers who serve honorably should be appropriately recognized before they depart the battalion. Exceptional performance will be recognized through the judicious use of impact awards. Team, crew, and unit awards will recognize collective efforts in sports or military skills competitions. The S1 will manage this program, which will be closely monitored by myself, the XO, and the CSM.

A note of caution: I view the battalion as a team, not a collection of competitive spirits. I value very highly subordinates' ability and willingness to work together, rather than against each other. You will have plenty of opportunities to compete against the established standard. If you have a good idea, share it and you'll move to the top of my list. You will see that I will take the same approach with other battalions in the brigade. We're all on the same team – let's be winners together.

l. **Non-negotiables**. There are a number of areas which I have little tolerance for. There are others which the Army views very unfavorably.

    i.   Breaches of integrity. Officers and NCOs hold a special trust. Violations of that trust by lying, cheating, stealing, or immoral behavior will rarely be forgiven. If you don't measure up, you don't belong in my Army.

ii. Lose a weapon. Don't come home without all of them. Conduct inventories by the book, both in garrison and in the field. If you lose one, report it immediately.

iii. Misappropriation of a government vehicle or property.

iv. Allowing a non-licensed driver to drive a military vehicle.

v. DUI – Know your limits and DON'T DRIVE when you reach them.

vi. Abuse or sale of drugs.

vii. Abuse of soldiers.

m. **Some Personal Quirks**. You need to understand some "peculiarities" or character traits of mine:

i. I value timeliness as an indicator of unit discipline and organization. If you are scheduled to start a range at 0800, don't fire the first round at 0830. If your SP is 0630, don't cross the LD at 0635. If you report REDCON 1, I expect you to react immediately when told to move. Failure indicates your inability to organize your time and discipline your unit.

ii. Attention to detail. Everything you do should be war-gamed and rehearsed, if only mentally. I will ask lots of questions to make sure you have thought all the way through a plan. Don't be insulted by this. I will insist on several layers of "checkers" for most major activities. It is not a sign of distrust, but rather an attempt to ensure all bases are covered.

iii. I value very highly persistence and initiative on the part of junior leaders. If you are "laid back" and indecisive, nothing will get done. It is easier to forgive a wrong decision than explain why none was made.

iv. When discussing an issue or problem with me, don't beat around the bush – get to the bottom line quickly. I begin to get impatient with long lead-ins, or what I perceive to be BS. State the problem up front and what you're doing about it.

v. In the same vein, I tend to give very detailed guidance if you let me. If you think you understand what I want, tell me early on, then update me periodically to ensure you are still on track. If you don't appear to grasp what I'm saying, I'll end up telling you what I want – and how to do it.

vi. I like to talk to the guy who has the action. Often this will be a supply clerk, armorer, or dispatcher. My experience has been that this is often the quickest and most accurate way of getting to the root cause of a problem. Don't take this as jumping the chain of command. I will try to include you when appropriate and you are available.

vii. Don't hide bad news. I won't shoot the messenger, and it doesn't get better with time. I'd rather know early on so we can fix it rather than wait and let it fester. Also, tell me before anyone on the brigade staff does.

2. Finally, unit identity is very important to me. I am very proud to be a soldier and am honored to be your commander. This is our battalion, not mine; I have only been given stewardship for the next two years. My regimental affiliation is with the 10th Cavalry, and there is nowhere else I would rather be. I look forward to a very challenging and rewarding two years. I'll do my best to ensure they are the same for you.

Craig B. Whelden
LTC, Armor
Commanding

Appendix B

Whelden on Whelden

Whelden on Whelden

I'm an ISTJ

- Serious, quiet, earn success by concentration and thoroughness
- Practical, orderly, matter-of-fact, logical, realistic, and dependable
- Takes responsibility
- Make up his own mind as to what should be accomplished and works toward it steadily, regardless of protest or distraction

The ISTJ Prayer

"God help me begin relaxing about the little details...

...tomorrow at 11:41:32 AM"

Whelden on Whelden

- I like to think I listen
- I don't shoot the messenger
- I'm not good with names and faces...but that doesn't mean I don't care
- I would rather direct/produce the play than star in it
- I haven't forgotten my roots...I've been there

Whelden on Whelden (cont.)

- I like the bottom line up front
- I like consensus...but encourage debate
- I think out loud...for the benefit of both of us
- I'm "low maintenance" but willingly accept help when it's beneficial to the process
- I like email
- IM, FM, Contracting, auditors and lawyers make my head hurt...but I'm glad they're here
- I like lawyers who help me figure out <u>HOW</u> I can do something rather than tell me why I can't, though I will always stay inside legal "boundaries"
- I'm not a technocrat or bureaucrat

Strengths <u>and</u> Weaknesses

- I'm low key...but some interpret this as not serious
- I really care...but it doesn't always show
- I like to "peel the onion back"...but I sometimes am too "dick and jane"
- I follow the rules...and... I follow the rules
- I tend to show all my cards...and... I tend to show all my cards
- I like to go straight to the A.O...but some interpret this as jumping the chain
- I'm a family man...so some probably think I'm boring

"We had trained well, but it seemed that every time we were beginning to form up into teams...we reorganized...

...I was to learn later in life that we tend to meet any new situation by reorganizing

...and a wonderful method it can be for creating the illusion of progress while producing confusion, inefficiency and demoralizing the troops..."

Attributed to Petronius Arbiter
Roman General, 66 AD

About the Author

C raig Whelden spent 30 years in the U.S. Army, followed by seven in the private sector, and another nine as a member of the Senior Executive Service (SES) with the U.S. Marine Corps.

Along the way, he led soldiers at each level from lieutenant to General Officer while serving 10 years in Europe and another 12 in the Pacific.

An Armor and Cavalry officer, he commanded a base in Germany as a colonel and, as a brigadier general, oversaw a $1.6B program supporting soldiers and family members world-wide.

Present at the Pentagon on 9/11, he subsequently led the effort to secure the state of Hawaii from terrorist attack, an effort that received national recognition. After retiring from the Army in 2003, he chaired a national conference on *Information Sharing and Homeland Security* for three years.

In 2008, he was asked to organize and run a Secretary of the Army initiative to bring greater awareness to the American public of the sacrifices of service-members and their families during a time of war. For this effort, he was recognized by Secretary Pete Geren with the top two awards for civilians.

In 2010, he became the Executive Director for Marine Corps Forces Pacific, overseeing a multi-billion-dollar program to reposition marines in the Pacific – the largest such effort since World War II.

In 2011, he was inducted into the Purdue University Tri-Service ROTC Hall of Fame.

Craig is a motivational speaker on leadership and performance excellence. He can be found on LinkedIn and reached at info@craigwhelden.com.

For more information and scheduling a speaking engagement, go to www.craigwhelden.com.